THIS BOOK
BELONGS TO

....

....

Thanks ever so much to each of my cherished readers for investing the time to read this book!

I know you could have picked from many other books, but you chose this one. So, a big thanks for reading all the way to the end. If you enjoyed this book or received value from it, I'd like to ask you for a favor. Please take a few minutes to **post an honest and heartfelt review on** Amazon.com. Your support does make a difference and helps to benefit other people.

Thanks!

©COPYRIGHT 2024

The content contained within this book may not be reproduced, duplicated, or transmitted without direct written permission from the author or the publisher. Under no circumstances will any blame or legal responsibility be held against the publisher, or author, for any damages, reparation, or monetary loss due to the information contained within this book. Either directly or indirectly.

Legal Notice:
This book is copyright protected. This book is only for personal use. You cannot amend, distribute, sell, use, quote, or paraphrase any part, or the content within this book, without the consent of the author or publisher.

Disclaimer Notice:
Please note the information contained within this document is for educational and entertainment purposes only. All effort has been executed to present accurate, up-to-date, and reliable, complete information. No warranties of any kind are declared or implied. Readers acknowledge that the author is not engaging in the rendering of legal, financial, medical, or professional advice. The content within this book has been derived from various sources. Please consult a licensed professional before attempting any techniques outlined in this book. By reading this document, the reader agrees that under no circumstances is the author responsible for any losses, direct or indirect, which are incurred as a result of the use of the information contained within this document, including, but not limited to — errors, omissions, or inaccuracies.

Table of Contents

INTRODUCTION	5
WHAT ARE BINARY OPTIONS	7
HISTORY OF BINARY OPTIONS AND THE IMPORT IN MONETARY MARKETS	10
HOW TO OPT FOR THE MOST EFFECTIVE BROKER	14
BINARY OPTIONS VS TRADITIONAL OPTIONS	18
DAY TRADING WAYS IN BINARY OPTIONS	20
HEDGING STRATEGY IN BINARY OPTIONS	23
12 TIPS FOR CHOSING BINARY OPTIONS BROKERS	26
WHY TRADE BINARY OPTIONS	29
LATEST NEWS AND COMPARISONS BETWEEN BINARY OPTIONS BROKERS	31
BANCE DI BINARY	33
GLOBAL CHOICE	34
STOP LOSS	35
HOW TO SET STOP LOSS	38
WHY TO USE CAUTION WITH TINY STOP LOSS	42
WHY TRADE WITH A STOP LOSS	45
METATRADER SUMMARY STOP LOSS AND TAKE PROFIT	53
TRADING WITH STOP LOSS AND TRAILING STOP	58
SEVEN COMMON STOP LOSS EXITS	60
FUNDAMENTAL VS TECHNICAL ANALYSIS	63
COMBINING TECHNICAL AND FUNDAMENTAL ANALYSIS	68
WHY TO IGNORE FUNDAMENTALS THROUGHOUT DAY TRADING	72
TRADING PSYCHOLOGY	74
SIX sensible TIPS TO MASTER MIND AND cash	83
RISK MANAGEMENT	88

INTRODUCTION

This book will help you to getting started.

It's a step-by-step guide to understand how trading works. You can learn a lot, starting from best strategies and tips to psychology that perform a very important role. I believe that this is the first fundamental pillar to make professional trading.

Everyone talks about profits but nobody tells you how a professional trader must behave against losses. This is the second fundamental pillar to make professional trading.

We will talk about risk management too, because it's the third fundamental pillar to make professional trading. We can also have other two pillars, strategies and psychology, but if we don't know how to manage our risk we will end up to loose everything.

Inside you will find:

-What options are and how they work

-What a stop loss and take profit are

-How much money you need to start

-Best profitable strategies that you should use in different scenarios

-What tools do you need

-What psychologically approach you should use

-The right mind-set you need to have to become a profitable trader

- How to manage your capital

- How to manage the risk

- Some tips to live long in markets

WHAT ARE BINARY OPTIONS

A binary option is a financial product where the buyer receives a payout or loses their investment, based on if the option expires in the money. Binary options depend on the outcome of a "yes or no" proposition, hence the name "binary." Binary options have an expiry date and/or time. At the time of expiry, the price of the underlying asset must be on the correct side of the strike price (based on the trade taken) for the trader to make a profit.

To make things a bit clearer, let's use Google shares as an example. Google shares, were being listed at around 880.23. A Binary trade on Google would allow the merchant a selection of whether or not Google shares would either go up or down. Inside a Binary options platform, the merchant would see a graph representing the Google share value for a set period of time. This value will appear along with two buttons and a graph. The buttons indicate the two selections of whether the option will go 'up' or 'down'.

In this example, the merchant chooses 'up', along with the termination of trade time sealed at 15 minutes from the execution of the trade. Once the time passes, the trade closes. If the value is greater than 880.23, the merchant has profited. If the value is lower the merchant has lost.

Are Binary options For You?

The first think to take into consideration is that with all investments, there's risk involved. Even as individuals can make a profit, they can also lose money. The most variations between Binaries and traditional trading are as follows:

• Options on a Binary platform are often listed quicker than typical trades.

- Costs on a Binary platform are invariably the mid-price, so there's no purchase or sell value. This implies that the instant change in the instrument moves within the direction of a trader's pre-selected selection, the merchant is instantly ahead on the trade.

- Binary option trades have immediate execution.

- Capital associated options trade are often created for as very little as $20.

- The returns on a Binary options trade are instant from the minute a trade has closed.

- There's no broker commission on the particular execution of the trade.

- The return relies upon the length of the termination time.

For traders who are accustomed to trading foreign currencies (FOREX), opening Binary options trades for currency pairs would be ideal. As mentioned, Binary options trades are solely ever quoted at middle rates. For a seasoned on-line Forex merchant, this implies that there's no pip unfold trading Forex in a very Binary Broker platform.

Learn Before You Trade

For new traders, before creating any call to speculate within the market, it's suggested to browse and find out about the markets, stocks and shares and the way volatile trading will typically become. It's vital to know what causes the changes in the markets direction. News for example affects the world's economy and therefore has different impacts on all of the markets.

Yahoo finance offers value quotes on each instrument that's listed inside a Binary options platform. The foremost common instruments are Forex, Commodities, Stocks and Shares. Till a possible merchant has a great degree of understanding of those instruments, it's not suggested to start out trading.

Additionally, one will browse on economic calendars. These are calendars that details forthcoming events like company announcements, major market changes and may provide insight into that direction a stock, Forex pair or goods are moving; that being whether they are going up or down.

For individuals who desire to trade inside a binary options platform, there are several factors that will influence your decision. However as much as you can learn about these, Magnum options for example, permits new users to open a Demo account and try out the the platform before creating any real cash deposits into a trading account.

HISTORY OF BINARY OPTIONS AND THE IMPORT IN MONETARY MARKETS

Financial instruments are major driving forces in today's finances. One among them is what's termed binary options. Binary options carry a high level of risks as it involves predicting the value of the percentage change, plus at a given period in time. Binary options are primarily 2 in nature: the cash-or-nothing choice and also the asset-or-nothing option. Whichever manner is chosen, if at the maturity of the worth isn't reached or the safety value is not earned, no binary payout are going to be received. options

Over-the-Counter amount

There was a time when trading was meted out only between the establishment and also the customer. This was for the most part thanks to the dearth or deficiency of liquid markets wherever these options may be listed before they'd expire. The official rules and rules that were used hitherto hardly applied to options. These were so referred to as over-the-counter binary options. They're currently distinguished from exchange listed binary options.

There is a distinction between over-the-counter commercialism and exchange trading. Whereas the previous bring into direct relation two parties, the latter needs the existence of well-organized structures and means that of commercialism referred to as exchange.

The advent of the commercialism Platforms

The year 2008 was a turning point in the history of options. So from that point binary options web-sites came up and stepped in to boost up exchange-traded all-or-nothing options. This development was timely because it was inside the spirit of the Securities and Exchange Commission (SEC)'s call to permit the listing of cash-or-nothing options. This was elicited by the proposal of the Options Clearing Corporation in 2007 to include binary options inside its rules.

Following the SEC's move the American exchange went full length for its 1st ever exchange-traded cash-or-nothing binary options. These were European trend options. What are their characteristics? The most important distinctive purpose of this trend is that it will solely be exercised at the expiration date. This is often in differentiation with the American trend which can be exercised before the termination date.

Emboldened by the options of the primary 2 regulative establishments, the Chicago Board Options Exchange (CBOE) launched an equivalent sort of options within the same year 2008. But in 1973 an equivalent CBOE created the mandatory facultative surroundings for options to be listed. It helped however it had been not broad enough. Besides, it was not open enough for several investors to seek out their share. However from their investment in options unbroken advancing until larger and stronger platforms were allowed to return up.

Additionally, in 2009 the North American Derivatives Exchange (Nadex) joined the bandwagon and began allowing digital options. Derivatives contracted over-the-counter are extraordinarily attractive: they attract low government taxation and create space for the payment of low fees. What is more the parties concerned will conceive to tailor the transactions as they consider work. Granted that the unlisted derivatives have some notable edges over the exchange listed derivatives, however Nadex understood the importance of keeping up with the dynamics of world finance that has thus well accommodated unlisted derivatives and given them a selection place within the world of trading.

If the world finance would live up to its name, the net should be allowed to interfere within the manner that binary options trading is completed. So currently several websites that supply on-line opportunities for trading have been developed and more are being developed.

According to recent statistics, roughly ninety binary options trading platforms are presently running. They set the order of the day by serving to alter the manner exchange listed binary options are being meted out.

Options Payoff Calculations

There are two ways in measuring payoff in binary options trading. They're labeled vanilla options and exotic options.

In vanilla options the payoff is calculated equally. Here the binary options are standardized in such a way that there's guarantee of continuous quotations. These options characterize exchange-traded contracts.

In exotic options, the payoff is calculated otherwise, there is no uniformity to the manner the binary options were exercised. Exotic options characterize unlisted contracts.

Growth Trend

The flexibility concerned in binary options trading has created the employment of those monetary instruments to skyrocket in a rare manner. Many people are excited at the likelihood of trading while not the compulsion of browsing the drafting and linguistic communication of some not-easy-to-figure-out contract. This wasn't the case with the standard trading pattern.

Indeed, with over-the-counter pattern the investment bank and also the shoppers agree by means that of a contract on the modalities of the longer-term settlement of a trade. However, on-line binary options innovated by dispensing traders from formal contract commercialism. Everyone is welcome, though it'll be wise to tread with caution. It's important to learn about the brokers and the trading platform you choose to trade with.

The Future is here!

The Internet has launched us into that future that we have access to things we once could only dream of. It's displayed additional prospects for investors within the monetary markets. It doesn't matter wherever you are in your expertise with options trading, you currently have the awe-inspiring chance to find out or improve on what you've got. The digital options trading has currently perforate into many economic and monetary sectors. The gambling trade isn't spared. Within the same vein, the prognosticative markets is creating use of the binary options. Fixed-odds gambling is running rampant online. Its need to do with political events, sporting events, weather et al. Technology is that driving force of the digital options trading. And as long as technology keeps developing, there looks to be no restraining issue (except modification of laws) to the explosion of the trade.

The attractiveness of this manner of trading could be a prelude to however bright the longer term of investors are going to be in this sector. They will still hope to relish all the advantages that it offers.

HOW TO OPT FOR THE MOST EFFECTIVE BROKER

Digital options trading is one among the foremost profitable investment opportunities obtainable within the market these days. Since the new market rules declared within the year 2008, the expansion of binary options trading has extremely catapulted and additional and more individuals are increasing their investments in binary options. Thanks to short term investments and better returns on those investments, Digital options trading has become one among the foremost standard market investment opportunities.

Investors will trade twenty four hours and seven days every week within the binary options market. At the same time, there's a harsh reality behind this sort of investment. One should have thorough data concerning these market trends to induce higher returns on their investments. This market is extremely dynamic and volatile in nature that indicates a powerful have to be compelled to keep constant eyes on the newest news and worldwide market happenings. Wherever a reliable and skilled binary options broker platform can facilitate investors to create simple and reliable trades mechanically.

How to opt for the most effective Binary options Broker?

Due to the continual rise within the quality of binary options trading opportunities, there's a growing demand for reliable and skilled binary options broker platforms. Sadly, there are many digital options broker platform that scams within the market and attempt to sell investors unreliable and untested binary options. This will cause severe losses to the traders thanks to the dearth of skilled and reliable binary commercialism computer code.

While choosing a reliable and skilled digital options broker program, one should inquire concerning the subsequent options and needs that each victorious binary trading computer code possess.

Important Binary options Broker options to keep in mind are:

1.) Easy and intuitive computer program

Skilled and reliable binary trading program offers simple and easy to handle user interface that saves heap of your time and headache for traders. One has to be compelled to invest time beyond regulation to find out new options and controls of the program. Most of those programs are net based mostly and users don't have to be compelled to transfer or update the trading computer code on their own computer. Users should be ready to use the program simply whenever and where they require. User friendly and interactive controls are the foremost vital ones that we should observe when choosing the proper binary options broker platform.

2.) Ability to speculate into multiple assets

Reliable and skilled binary trading computer code offers types of assets for the investment purpose. A merchant ought to be ready to invest into differing types of market assets from Forex, indices to stocks and commodities. One should concentrate on the power of the program to speculate into all of the obtainable market assets to realize most profits from the trades.

3.) Accessibility of acceptable termination periods

Some binary trading brokers give weekly expiry periods whereas some provide hourly and end of the day options to their investors. To realize most management on our trades, it's vital to pick the binary trading computer code that has most termination periods.

4.) Most payout share

Skilled and standard digital options brokers give maximum payout percentage to their investors. One should look into the binary trading platform which will supply minimum seventy fifth to ninetieth payout share for each won and lost investment. For each unsuccessful trade, there should be minimum five-hitter to 100 percent returns to the traders.

5.) Types of languages offered

To become apt with the usage of the binary trading computer code, it's essential that the language of the program should be your own first language. There are some skilled binary options broker platforms within the market that provide types of languages from English, Arabic, Spanish, Russian, Turkish, etc.

6.) Minimum initial deposit needs

One should be ready to open binary trading account at the website for complimentary and not be compelled to give initial deposits. Seek for those binary trading platforms that give free registrations and lowest deposits.

7.) Types of payment options

skilled binary options trading platforms give varieties of payment strategies like PayPal, bank transfer, Mastercard, etc. seek for such binary or digital options broker that provide multiple sorts of payment withdrawal options.

8.) Higher bonuses

Some digital options broker worship to twenty fifth bonuses to their traders that conjointly rely upon total turnover and initial deposit quantity from the traders. Seek for such trading platforms that provide higher bonuses to their users.

9.) Top notch client support

Top quality customer service is equally vital to induce timely support and help throughout every type of trades. Skilled digital trading brokers and platforms invariably give client support in types of languages and via multiple platforms like email, live chat, and phone support.

BINARY OPTIONS VS TRADITIONAL OPTIONS

The distinction between binary options vs traditional options is in its trade structure. Though there are variations they're conjointly similar in many ways. Underlying assets are listed in each markets and that they have a planned termination amount or date that's determined before inserting a trade. The various kinds of assets that are traded in each of the markets are similar with some assets unlisted within the binary market.

Binary options

• It's a straightforward and structured manner of trading wherever traders play 2 doable outcomes in a trade.

• The merchant could also be ready to get a set come as all trades should attend the termination amount before the result is set.

• In binary options the traders are obliged to exercise the choice after they expire.

In this market, complicated price quotation systems don't exist and instead, traders could gauge the performance of the trade that they had placed. You'll not be ready to purchase the plus at a later date during this market.

• The merchant is ready to create profit during this market counting on however the underlying plus moves throughout the choice amount.

• The profit or loss in binary is mounted whereas the profits in ancient market are tiny.

- You'll be ready to increase the profit once you perceive the trend of the plus before you place a trade.

- The same as traditional options, binary can even be listed in monthly increments. But the trades are placed in increments that vary from quarter-hour to one hour.

Traditional options

- The option is sometimes exercised counting on what quantity the plus has gained in worth. You'll be able to opt for many ways that of trading once you choose the standard technique.

As a merchant you'll conjointly like better to shut the trade early. They'll not be ready to do thus in binary options. Some brokers have started giving the choice of early advance binary and this allows the merchant to hedge.

- Compared to the binary options market, the standard options market is additional risky.

- Leverage, margin needs and bigger commissions increase the chance better in the standard market.

As trade payouts are displayed before execution in binary market they need reduced risks to the merchant. This will facilitate in minimizing the losses simply.

After you become tuned in to the fundamental distinction between binary options vs ancient options, you'll be able to opt for any sort of investment choice you wish counting on your individual trading preference.

DAY TRADING WAYS IN BINARY OPTIONS

An increase within the quantity of assorted binary options trading ways is capably mirrored from the recognition of binary options trading inside the recent months. With high profit potential, low entry deposits, the binary trading trade has been boosted to the extent that speculators currently actively ask for binary trading options strategies to assist maximize their profits farther. Loads of the options trading techniques are typically developed by binary options capitalists and monetary professionals to readily assist the investor by giving them a trading advantage within the ever volatile stock markets.

Day trading in binary options is seen as a strictly speculative driven markets that also brings concerning the amount of challenges involved it yet. With a rise of challenges, comes the demand for a decent binary options strategy that will offset the threats conferred by the risky markets, specifically throughout time once the markets will flip either manner. The recognition of options trading along with the speedy profits that are made from the markets and also the assumptive nature, will build it a robust investment tool. There are many various strategies that are supported the binary options markets, so we have a tendency to shed lightweight on many.

Choosing each decision and place choice maneuver

The thrill provided by the speculative markets is that the more and more standard binary options trading strategy enforced by binary options investors who typically throughout a trade acknowledge that the option they opt for can find yourself trading out-of-the-money. Typically, this is often where the story ends for several investors. Taking associate degree example, of associate degree capitalist who has purchased a USD100 purchase an end-of day decision choice on the FTSE100 index at a strike value of USD1.1800 and notices that the trade goes against what the capitalist speculated, one among the foremost simplest strategy in binary option is usually to get a place choice of an equivalent initial invested with worth that is USD100. Selecting this type of a method that has trades in opposite directions, investors will minimize their losses.

Benefiting from winning trades

This strategy is sometimes referred to as increasing the trade and is often employed in binary options trading. Taking for example of a forex merchant who invested USD100 place option on the FTSE100 at ten.033, the capitalist realizes that the trade goes in his profit and trading below the ten.033 level, the trader can buy an extra option within the same direction, so increasing their prospects to realize from the trades. The advantages of victimization this type of strategy is that traders will build extraordinarily high financial gain from their initial investments. This sort of a method, although easy on paper involves a small amount of legwork and numerous factors that establish the results of the trade. For starters, once you place your next trade an equivalent direction, a very important issue that plays a task is that the time for termination. As a worst-case situation, if the primary trade is thanks to finish within the next quarter-hour and you open a second trade an equivalent direction, there's an opening that the markets are doubtless to retract inside the timeframe of termination of your second trade.

The event technique

The concept of the market pull strategy is to get in either a decision or place option based mostly upon forceful imbalances of costs within the markets. For instance, once you concentrate on the market or economic news that hints at a government call which may lower the currency worth, a binary options trader might purchase a place choice of the currency combine, like EUR/USD. What justifies this trading decision is that the conviction that the news printed shows signs of decreasing the price of the currency pair. Using such maneuver associate degree capitalist will build massive profits.

Unlimited potential

The techniques various binary options traders have adopted influenced by their trading expertise. The key to developing or applying an efficient trading strategy lies within the indisputable fact that with due specialize in info and perseverance, investors might presumably keep income by trading binary options. You'll notice inherent challenges concerned within the method, through experimenting, although with trial and error and ensuring you don't find yourself losing all of your investment, binary options that includes its high winnings and quick results and also the mounted challenges they create, traders will build up an oversized portfolio in a very short period of time.

HEDGING STRATEGY IN BINARY OPTIONS

Binary options strategy techniques:

Binary options trading is earning loads of recognition among marketers, as it's associate degree exciting and new trading technique. several of the traders victimization completely different ways, however the fundamental construct of all binary options ways are an equivalent and in contrast to different professions, the binary options trading provides solely 2 doable results, the gain or loss.

According to the binary selection strategy guide, there are some ways that are basic and are followed by all traders. Therefore, if you follow a decent strategy for binary choice, you'll be ready to get smart yields.

• The primary of those ways is that the link for the "a" within the decision cash and also the money placed. Therefore, whether or not at maturity, the terms is between the 2 costs, you'll be able to still earn cash. Another strategy that's helpful within the operations of binary selection, because it can assist you to link the post with a decision to a weasel-worded position and doubles. This binary selection strategy is additionally helpful in creating profits.

• Another quite common strategy, that most of the traders use whereas trading is that the binary indulgent options strategy. During this strategy, the traders can build run-option, once there's associate degree surprising giant fluctuation within the market. Binary indulgent options strategy will facilitate the individuals to place in positions that influence the indications of market costs in a very massive manner. As example, the quarterly of the businesses on their profits or losses are determined with nice enthusiasm by the merchants, as a result of the movement of stock costs of those firms is affected thanks to the positive or negative. Likewise, the declared plans and different events which will influence markets, like natural disasters and political modification are viewed by traders.

When to use hedging strategy using binary options?

However, if you're hedging using the binary option, there are several things, that you've got to think about. Below listed are a number of these things:

Identifying the risks: the choice to hedge or not depends in the main on the risks that the corporate is exposed. However, a rigorously designed hedging strategy reduces prices and risks. Correct use of ways for binary options on the coverage of this type will facilitate merchants defend themselves and maximize their profit.

Hedging ways using binary options:

Hedging could be a strategy that's utilized by individual operators to scale back investment risk through numerous strategies like shopping for and trading options, promoting techniques or futures contracts within the short term. The hedging ways are designed to scale back volatility associate degreed potential risk of a portfolio or an investment to reduce the chance of loss. Basically, there's the advantage of block existing edges. Hedging ways are used most often, whereas Forex trading and binary option are used together with hedging ways to reduce the chance of loss.

For some time currently, binary options trading are used for daily transactions. Though it should sound strange, a merchandiser who features a thorough data of binary options are often used for partial coverage. It conjointly provides a chance to reap additional profits.

The rational use of decision and place options will cut back risks any. In fact, profits are often double-binary options if dead properly.

As a trader, understand that the bulk of binary options trades ended at the top of the day or each hour. If the value of a specific action, i.e. $20 and may build a profit of $200, currently if costs rise as his prediction in associate degree hour before it expires, you've got the choice of whether or not to carry or sell the quota before the expiration. The choice to retain the fee depends on several factors. The longer term depends on market and different sources of data that helps traders analyze the market.

Now, during this specific case, you'll be able to use partial or full coverage. Full coverage involves the sale of all shares during this situation. This could bring edges within the given time. Partial coverage means to retain some shares, whereas trading a number of them. Though there's some risk connected as trade, to some extent still is open, however risk losing the shares sold-out is reduced. If at the time of expiration, the trader's prediction is correct, would have the profit, however while not involving any risk.

12 TIPS FOR CHOSING BINARY OPTIONS BROKERS

Taking a read the finance pool are often terribly exciting, however it can even be terribly intimidating and downright alarming. Another to capital punishment the binary trades yourself is to rent binary options brokers. There are several brokers within the trade prepared and willing to figure with you or in your position and perform the trading tasks for you. The downside to hiring a broker isn't all brokers are right for all investors. Here, are some tips to assist opt for your best broker.

What client Service Do They Offer?

1. Binary options brokers receive a fee if your trade loses. Some brokers need a trading fee when they execute a dealings. If a broker needs each fees, confirm the full of the 2 is inside an affordable rate, like ten you must 15 August 1945. Most of them are useful, however that doesn't mean they must receive the Lion's share of the success.

2. Client service could be a thought once selecting brokers. They must be obtainable by a well-liked means that like email, phone calls and live chat. You actually don't wish to miss out on an awfully profitable deal as a result of you'll not contact client service. Client service ought to even be obtainable in your language of selection.

3. Seek for binary options brokers who supply some refund if the trade doesn't build any cash. Some brokers can do this, however on condition that asked. Confirm the refund is affordable like 15 August 1945 of the cash lost. This is often a decent incentive for the broker to offer your account its due focus.

Do they need acceptable Technology?

4. The platform used ought to be web-based and not a program transfer. This can offer you the power to see on your investments once in a very whereas, yet as being assured the newest version of the trading program is getting used. The program and your account ought to be simple to access with no hidden aspects of the account. Confirm your account is out there in your linguistic communication or no matter language you select.

5. Brokers that are depletion up to now technology can have a system in situ that enables you to use your smart phone to have interaction within the commercialism method or to only check your account. If that's a very important thought, take care the broker of selection has that choice obtainable

6. If multiple trading options are vital for your investment portfolio, opt for brokers that have that ability yet as computer code in situ that accommodates such a call for participation. There's a range of binary options computer code obtainable and a few of the programs are binary options solely, however there are many others that have many capabilities designed into one platform.

7. Confirm binary options brokers use the newest technology to safe guard your info from hackers and fraud. Hackers are close to in step with technology and also the importance to create certain your info is protected can't be stressed enough. Don't permit others to own access to your account aside from binary options brokers and confirm your broker of selection will an equivalent.

8. The broker of selection ought to keep all of your account info in one place for straightforward review. All the past assets and transactions and people being dead within the gift ought to even be open for review and in a straight forward to seek out place. This makes it simple to review past trends and appearance at the various trades below sure trading conditions.

Do they meet your expectations?

9. Payment and withdrawal options are invariably a very important thought once selecting brokers. Customers typically wish to utilize a unique and convenient family planning like Mastercard or bank transfer to create the initial investment and withdraw payments through PayPal or another industry. Brokers that provide a range of options can presumably use the tactic you favor. If they're tied to 1 payment and family planning, chances are high that they aren't the binary options brokers for you.

10. Monetary transactions between you and binary options brokers ought to be as immediate as doable. The broker demands his cash for every dealings in a very timely manner, and you must be offered an equivalent thought. If payment to you lags for 3 business days, it would be time to seek out different binary options brokers.

11. Confirm your broker has associate degree education section on their data processor that enables customers to find out concerning binary options trading. The additional info the client has, the higher they will work with and perceive what the brokers do.

12. Before linguistic communication on the line and entrusting your monetary future to binary options brokers, perceive their terms and conditions and the other written agreement live they need in situ.

WHY TRADE BINARY OPTIONS

Binary options are a straightforward and appreciated monetary trading product. They deliver a set return on each trade that's created, supported whether or not the trade was "In the Money", "Out Of the Money" or maybe a "Tie". Binary options (also referred to as digital options or BO for short) - tend to be one among the quickest growing monetary trading product on the planet as a result of their comfort, along with using the amount of knowledge that they supply on each trade, makes them a attractive trading tools for quite an few monetary investors.

When getting a binary options the potential homecoming it offers is for certain yet as notable before purchasing is formed. Digital options are often purchased on just about any monetary product and may be purchased in directions of trade presumably by shopping for a "Call"/"Up" choice or a "Put"/"Down" option. This implies that trader are long or instead short on any monetary item just by shopping for a binary choice. They're offered against a set termination period of time that might feel e.g. 5-30 hour within the future, associate degree hour close to forward or at the shut of every trading evening. Once digital options are purchased, they can't be resold till termination time is up.

Trading digital options is extremely standard among traders only if it's very easy and will generate high returns in brief time. Completely different from classical trading precisely wherever every purpose features a sure blessings that's proportional to the amount listed, in binary options you simply need to predict the proper movement for a set amount of your time. If you recognize the market can presumably form within the next half-hour, you purchase a decision choice and you get seventy fifth come in your investment. It doesn't matter if the market touched solely by ten units or by seventy units, the profit is that the very same. This may well be why they generate the very best profits of all types of trading.

A positive facet of binary options trading is that the indisputable fact that you'll be able to build terribly sturdy ways and cash management techniques, thanks to its binary character. You'll be able to build terribly precise calculations of your financial gain according so as to the amount of trades and also the winning quantitative relation. You probably will follow some specific values and build the steady profit.

Because of simply however they work, you in theory would like a five hundredth probability so as to predict the proper outcome whether or not or not you don't build any quite analysis. A straightforward uneducated guess can still have five hundredth winning possibilities (buying options with none info otherwise study will understand as binary gaming). Currently imagine what quantity cash you'll be able to build if for instance the study takes your winning fee to 70%!

LATEST NEWS AND COMPARISONS BETWEEN BINARY OPTIONS BROKERS

A binary option in its easy language is understood as investment vehicle. Its associate degree all or nothing investment. Binary commercialism could be a lucid trading resource that has gained large fame and is useful for each tiny and enormous investors willing to create beautiful financial gain while not substantial expertise and data of binary options bet markets. Because the term binary suggests, it's solely 2 doable outcomes that are, either profit or no profit in any respect if the speculation goes wrong. Initially, this may sound complicated and unattractive, however the subsequent pointers concerning the terribly commencement of binary options trading can build a major distinction in your business.

Binary options Brokers Play a major Role in Your Binary options Business

Binary trade brokers are the professionals of binary bet markets of commodities, stocks events and indices, round the world. They use their experience within the field to assist the traders and help them in earning optimum payout. Several of the brokers work as affiliate of assorted firms. Typically, a number of the binary brokers advocate a platform to use, or reveal various helpful tips about binary trading. Whereas, others concentrate on completely different goods assets like petroleum, gold, silver, forex, pharmaceutical firms etc. However, brokers can even concentrate on indices that are a range of various commodities or stocks. Usually, once the traders and consultants (brokers) return up to a typical ground associated with derivatives, they start the business with finding out the actual underlying plus. This method could embody browsing numerous articles, websites, reports, monetary tools etc. once an in depth study, modeling of anticipated costs is given a priority.

As a newcomer within the binary trading business, you'll notice the data of consultants terribly helpful. While not associate degree expert's support, you may not access the proper quite knowledge and knowledge from reliable sources. As associate degree capitalist, it's equally vital to dig out the candidate among all the obtainable brokers thus on take care concerning the safety of your investments. Below are the precise and transient background details of 2notable binary options brokers.

BANCE DI BINARY

It is a virtual binary options broker. It's essentially a bank that permits its account holders to trade binary choice. It had been established in 2009 in the Big Apple with the efforts of toughened team of pros. up to now it's the foremost reliable and trustworthy platform to start business with. The platform constitutes the foremost informative material so as to serve the newcomers in binary trading. They assist to apprentice the behavior of monetary market totally. The foremost charming feature of this broker is their easy interface, with associate degree addition of demo account. The high level of convenience in trading, provides this platform a position over others. Moreover, this platform has been endued with best client service award within the recent years. The convenience of gap associate degree account in 3 currencies particularly, USD, monetary unit and JPY conjointly play a significant role in its quality. Lastly, the dedication of the team has created it one among the leading binary options commercialism whole worldwide. With the assistance of this platform, you'll be able to trade confidently.

GLOBAL CHOICE

This trading platform was conjointly launched in 2009, benefiting day traders, investors, and brokers globally. Most significantly, it provides you the payout of concerning seventy you look after your investment. It's a straightforward and manageable platform, and doesn't would like any computer code to initiate trading. The sweetness of this platform lies within the kind of binary trading options. You'll be able to experience live trading situation whereas getting numerous digital choice contracts for currencies, commodities, stocks and different quite eighty various underlying assets. The foremost feature of this binary broker is that the usage of latest binary options commercialism tools. These tools, without a doubt, help traders create precise speculation on value movements. Moreover, this platform has not in any respect neglected the importance of risk management, and has enclosed numerous involved tools such imposition, Buy-Me-Out to maximize the profit and minimize the chance at the same time.

STOP LOSS

When volatility is high and stocks move up and down, does one understand when to put a stop loss? Is there a right distance from the stock's value to place the stop loss? Is there an accurate procedure to see where to put it? Because the stock approaches the stop loss, you'll get nervous and wish to cancel the stop loss that the stock won't be sold-out. However, does one keep from trading timely or from obtaining "psyched" out of a decent stop loss (as once emotions cause someone to second-guess reason) and staying with a nasty position too long? The solution to the primary queries is expounded to answer the last question. If your stop loss placement is mathematically sound and supported by the laws of chance, and you really perceive and settle for what meaning, you won't be as simply psyched out. That's a significant advantage of a volatility stop loss. It's supported mathematically determined significance. An equivalent are often aforementioned for stop losses supported support levels. A breakdown through a price is of significance.

Getting "psyched out" could be a psychological downside that always gets within the manner of disciplined finance. Once, I was managing accounts on behalf of our informative firm, a shopper asked if it wouldn't be a decent plan to own stop-losses in situ to guard America if any of our stocks plunged. I had simply taken the positions and had not placed the stops. At the time, that stop-losses would be acceptable. I had been teaching shoppers for several months concerning the necessity to implement a stop loss for each position. The teachings apparently were sinking in. Here could be a special Bulletin: any individual who doesn't use stop losses is mendicancy to be schooled a lesson in risk management. The market can oblige.

There are those that firmly believe risk management however get "psyched out" of their discipline by the market. For instance, someone may attempt to use a stop-loss then hand over on stop-losses altogether once that stop is triggered simply before the stock resumes its climb. The foundation of the stop-loss "problem" is that the uncertainty that stems from most people's lack of information relating to correct stop placement. They either place the stop too far-off from the stock, or the opposite and thus close just about guaranteed to be triggered.

If a stock repeatedly rebounds once a decline to $50, then there's support at $50. Meaning there's demand at that level. If the stock drops through that value, it means that the commercialism was severe enough that it overpowered all the consumers at that level. That's a major event. Slightly below that purchasing support is wherever a stop loss belongs. If the stock breaks through that support, it's destined to go lower. Our own traders seek for vital events like this and that they conjointly look for events that are statistically significant. That is, once stock behavior is outside the traditional distribution of excursions for that stock, it's thought of vital. Here is associate degree example. If it's traditional for a stock to create excursion of up to twenty on either aspect of a 50-day moving average inside an amount of one hundred days, then excursion of three below the moving average would be vital. Refusing to sell on a major negative event won't stop the decline. It'll solely price you cash. Individuals don't prefer to admit they're wrong. They take hold the hope that the stock can eventually live up to expectations.

Assume that the distribution of a stock's daily low costs concerning its moving average indicates that downward valueexcursions adequate or bigger than four-dimensional below the stock's moving average occur just the once in two hundred days. Assume that you are attempting to capture the gains achieved by trends that last concerning one hundred days. A spike of four-dimensional below the moving average would be outside the chance envelope of your investment time-horizon (the stock is deviating way more than is "normal" for the stock). That sort of value excursion would be a major event. That's wherever a stop loss belongs. It might be foolish to stay holding the stock and hoping for a recovery. To try and do thus would be blatant proof of a scarcity of discipline. A disciplined merchant would sell like a shot. although the merchant ought to later conceive to repurchase a stock recently sold-out, the choice are going to be supported a lot of bigger clarity of thought and with additional sound judgment once it's sold-out than the decision to retain a stock that's already within the portfolio.

Of course, the caller mentioned on top of knew the stock was at an occasional by discernment. If the stock continues to fall, the caller would have thought the move was well-timed. The purpose is that at any given moment one will ne'er be 100 percent certain what a stock can do next. One among the most important errors a merchant or capitalist will build is to confuse what's with what is hoped for or with what has been. The most effective traders invariably keep their eyes on this. Functioning on what's (on what the facts really are within the present) typically means that relinquishing your preconceptions concerning what a stock needs to do. If a stock has broken through support, ditch your expectations for the stock. The corporate could also be nice and its product may be marvelous, however its stock is for a few different time.

HOW TO SET STOP LOSS

Why Set a Stop Loss?

If you'd prefer to savvy to be a forex merchant then the primary factor you need to understand is that forex product are generally listed on margin accounts with giant amounts of leverage, sometimes anyplace from 50:1 to 200:1 and typically as high as 500:1. Leverage are often a good tool permitting the employment of a comparatively bit of cash so as to exploit the unsteady worth of an oversized amount of money. This can also work against you because the unsteady worth of an oversized amount of cash can cause you to lose all of the comparatively bit of money. This comparatively bit of cash is your capital that's deposited with the broker and will not really be a little amount of money. This is often why you need to use correct risk management techniques when trading to guard your capital. The foremost basic of risk management techniques is using the forex stop loss order. This assigns a limit to the number of loss which will be taken on a private trade, however what quantity loss is acceptable?

Acceptable Loss

Acceptable loss is relative to several things but a decent place to start out is to appear at the particular worth of one unit of loss. Profits and losses are measured in units referred to as PIPs that are documented from the fourth decimal place in most quotes. For instance, if you were to shop for EURUSA for one.3471 and sell it for one.3465 then you'd have taken a loss of six pips. Forex product are sold-out in quantities of tons. a regular heap or one.0 heap is for one hundred,000 units, a mini heap or zero.1 heap is for one0,000 units and a small heap or zero.01 heap is for one,000 units. The particular worth of every pip is relative to the scale of the heap you've got ordered. Using EURUSA one.3471, to shop for a regular heap or one.0 heap, you'd have to pay one.3471USD * one hundred,000 units for a complete of $134,710USD for one hundred,000EUR before applying leverage. Since a pip is measured as zero.0001, the subsequent calculation are often created ((.0001 / 1.3471) * one hundred,000) which supplies a pip worth of seven.4234EUR. In USA bucks this could be seven.4234EUR * one.3471 (exchange rate) and provides $10USD per pip. Pip values in America bucks will merely be declared as being $10 for a regular heap or one.0 heap of one hundred,000 units, $1 for a mini heap or zero.1 heap of one0,000 units, and $0.10 for a small heap or zero.01 heap of one,000 units. Thus for the instance of a six pip loss, if you've got listed with a regular heap then your loss would be $60 or with a mini lot you'd have lost $6 and a loss of $0.60 with a small heap.

Give Loss a price

Now that you know what to expect for a unit of loss, you'll be able to provide the most allowable loss a price supported what quantity capital you've got to speculate. A decent worth for a beginner to start out with is a pair of your total capital for any one trade. This implies that if you've got $1000 to speculate then a a pair of loss would equate to $20. If you were to travel with a regular heap that features a pip worth of $10USD then you'll solely lose a pair of pips before most loss. You wish to permit loss while not closing your position along with your stop loss directly so a regular heap would be large for your capital level. A decent start line is to permit a loss of fifty pips before your forex stop loss order is triggered. A mini heap with a pip worth of $1USD is obtaining nearer because it would yield twenty pips before your most loss is reached, however still not ideal for a beginner. A small heap comes with a pip worth of $0.10USD permitting two hundred pips loss before most allowable loss is reached. If we have a tendency to take two hundred pips and divide by four the result's fifty pips thus currently take the 0.01 heap and multiply by four to induce zero.04 that tells America that zero.04 tons or four x zero.01(micro lot) could be a smart quantity to order with a stop loss of fifty pips. Simply keep in mind to stay with currency pairs that have enough active trades so your stop loss order are often stuffed once it's triggered. If the broker cannot fill your order thanks to lack of trade volume on the currency combined then losses could continue on the far side of your most allowable quantity till the order are often stuffed. Staying with the most important currency pairs can eliminate this doable downside. The majors are EURUSD, USDJPY, GBPUSD, AUDUSD, USDCHF, and USDCAD.

Trailing Stop Loss

If you're searching for forex commercialism ways that employment, strive a sophisticated technique used with a stop loss order referred to as trailing stop loss. This offers you the power to scale back or eliminate the likelihood of any loss by moving your stop loss quantity with the increasing profit of your order. Once your combine features a profit of fifty pips you'll be able to move your 50 pip stop loss quantity to your price or break-even purpose that the worse you can do is reach on your trade. You'll be able to take this one step any and still follow the increasing worth of your trade and guarantee profits. Your trade terminal can presumably supply this as an automatic feature. This is often a 1manner strategy and you must ne'er modification your stop loss worth within the negative direction in the hope that your trade can recover if it solely had many further pips of loss to figure with. Setting a stop loss on order sizes that employment along with your level of capital can prevent from losing all the cash you've got designed with profitable trades on one massive loss. Don't be greedy, attempt to keep feeling out of the equation, never invest cash that you just cannot afford to lose and you'll be one step nearer to trading Forex for a living on a beach somewhere that has Wi-Fi.

WHY TO USE CAUTION WITH TINY STOP LOSS

In the past, many traders had lot of loses trades unlike their expectations. The cause was a superficial triviality - too tiny stop-loss. Let me explain why this will be a drag, what to bear in mind and the way to avoid this danger. The subsequent topic is simply concerning those flight ways that are using purchase order to open a foothold and, at an equivalent time, they're using too tiny stop-loss (this article isn't concerning ways using market order). What's too tiny stop-loss? Well, it depends on the market and also the timeframe. However generally, it's a stop-loss smaller than the scale of a median bar of our main timeframe. Let me offer you an example - if we have a tendency to be employing a 30-minute chart with a median bar worth 250 USD, associate degreed our strategy is functioning with an eighty USD stop-loss, we have a tendency to be heading into a significant hassle. The live trade results may (and in most cases nearly most likely will) be whole completely different from those who we've got from the rear take a look at. Let's take a glance at the explanation why.

This downside happens once the stop-loss is thus tiny, that a number of the trades have entry order and stop-loss on an equivalent bar. Let's say we've got entry purchase order on the value one hundred and a stop-loss on the price ninety-nine . Now, imagine that the bar opens on ninety eight.7, it goes to one hundred.1 and that we open the long position - and also the stop-loss is ready up to ninety nine. And every one of this happens inside an equivalent bar - i.e. inside this one bar, the entry order is activated, the position is opened and also the stop-loss is ready up.

Now it's vital to know why this will be without a doubt a dangerous downside. It's quite easy. There are many back testing platforms that don't seem to be ready to acknowledge, with the incorrect setup or once the information resolution isn't fine enough if the stop-loss was or wasn't hit on associate degree entry bar. In different words, there are sure thing once, in reality, the stop-loss was hit right once the position was opened, as a result of right once the activation of the entry order, the market starts heading south. However, our back testing platform evaluates the trade as a profitable.

Let's continue with the demonstration of matters represented. During this state of affairs we will see the rising bar, i.e. the one that features a shut value on top of open price and, at an equivalent time, the shut is getting ready to its high. There's associate degree assumption that the bar was raising the entire time and also the broker assumes that the "inner" move of the bar, i.e. the manner the bar was generated, was perpetually rising, a line.

The broker is solely following the logic that once the bar closed getting ready to its high, the method of generating this bar was rising. In such state of affairs, the broker assumes that the bar opened on ninety eight.7 and also the value was unendingly rising to one hundred.4. And through now, it conjointly activated our purchase order on the value one hundred.

Nevertheless, this is often terribly inaccurate and dangerous assumption. What if the bar was 1st rising, activated our order, then again it reversed and went go into reverse, below our stop-loss, and so started rising once more to shut to its high?

This is a completely realistic situation that's happening every day which would end in a transparent loss (right once we have a tendency to open the position) - and however, the broker (and doubtless conjointly different software), defines matters as if there wasn't any correction within the bar in any respect. Thus no stop-loss was hit and trade terminated up as a profitable one. this is often the foundation cause to major issues as within the back take a look at you clearly see loads of profitable trades that, in reality, would find yourself as losses - and right once we have a tendency to begin trading this strategy live, everything starts falling apart...

Protection

The first protection against this threat is easy and, to a particular level, extremely economical. The broker calls it LIBB (Look-Inside-Bar-Back testing), others use completely different names, like Bar scientific instrument. the purpose is that once you activate this feature, the program appearance within the bar to the amount of the best obtainable knowledge resolution (in most cases it's one minute), if there wasn't any within correction once the entry order was activated, or if there was a correction on an equivalent bar after we entered and also the stop-loss was hit.

Despite that it feels like a good resolution (which is these days a regular a part of most platforms), it doesn't need to be sufficient once it involves tiny stop-losses. Why? Imagine a state of affairs once your stop-loss is USD $80, however the common bar of your finest LIBB resolution (i.e. principally one minute) is a hundred and fifty USD massive. In this case you're experiencing an equivalent downside as represented on top of, once the platform isn't ready to confirm whether or not the stop-loss within the bar was hit or not and it makes, again, simply associate degree inaccurate approximations that are driven by the above-described logic - if the bar closed nearer to its low or closer to its high. In different words, you're once more at the start and with too small stop-loss, not even LIBB can assist you, and also the downside still persists.

WHY TRADE WITH A STOP LOSS

There are a pair of sorts, if we have a tendency to place a sell order then we want to put a stop loss at a particular distance on top of our entry value. If we have a tendency to place a purchase order we want to put a stop loss at a particular distance below our entry value. For instance let's say on EURUSD the value is at one.22432 and that we wish to sell thus, if we wish a twenty pip stop loss. We have a tendency to place it at one.22632.

Using a stop loss in this case could be a method of solely risking a little quantity of generally between 1 Chronicles - five-hitter of our total commercialism capital per trade. And thence conjointly limiting the losses on our account that puts our minds at rest once commercialism. The foremost vital part of trading is science or place differently it's concerning however you react to it value once it triggers your signal. Or place differently it'll have an effect on however you perform as a merchant.

When I trade I sometimes risk concerning twenty pips per trade. This implies if I'm commercialism at $1 per pip then my risk is $20 and means I might would like a complete bank of $400 if I used to be to feel comfy taking that trade. I wouldn't feel comfy if I used to be risking any further than that and if I don't feel comfortable then it'll have an effect on my commercialism actions. for instance I'd hesitate and acquire in late, or if I see profit however I'm afraid I'd take profit but this might suffocate a very smart trade. So, as we have a tendency to understand obtaining a stop loss at tier were comfy with is extremely vital for your science that overall will have an effect on your commercialism selections which is able to affect your performance. A bit like any sport to it matter.

It's typically detected it being aforementioned that "a true skilled merchant doesn't care if he wins or loses". Well this is often true as a result of he is aware of his technique of commercialism can terribly most likely herald profit over the long run. What's vital is what percentage trades we have a tendency to win compared to how many we lose and you will slowly understand this over time. Thus this is often why whether or not you win or lose if you're a real skilled it merely doesn't matter on one specific day. It's once we have a tendency to losing over several months that tells America we aren't doing well and wish to re-evaluate things.

BUT don't think about stop loss techniques alone to create a profitable system!

It's a subject matter of a lot of discussion I'm certain on precisely however you utilize a stop and I'm sure there's additional books and websites out there giving much scope on this subject however as way as I see a real long run profitable commercialism system though I might say desires a stop loss and is extremely vital. It shouldn't think about a stop loss technique to be profitable as I'm certain it won't work long run as sometimes these kinds of system find yourself wiping out your entire capital once things fail.

A good commercialism system should get the direction right the bulk of the time otherwise its wishing on the stop technique that in my read isn't the trail to long run profitable trading. Let's take Roulette as associate degree example. Now, I'm a disciple of on-line roulette however I can tell you from expertise there's no system which will beat roulette despite what you are doing. There are I've detected over 7000 roulette systems out there. Of them there'll be variations of these that think about a indulgent technique referred to as Martingale. Let's shortly explain:

Martingale essentially aims to recoup a loss by doubling consequent bet. The attract is robust and quite justly as thus it seems you'll be able to lose however Buckeye State affirmative you can. You see eventually an extended run can wipe out the chance capital of the player. If you look into the roulette player from short term then it'll seem they're doing well however if you look at their taking part in over several months they are terribly doubtless to own lost their entire working capital at some purpose.

Example:

Balance $100

Bet $1 on Red it Loses Balance = $99

Bet $2 on Red it Wins Balance = $101

Bet $1 on Red it Wins Balance = $102

Bet $1 on Red it Loses Balance = $101

Bet $2 on Red it Loses Balance = $99

Bet $4 on Red it Loses Balance = $95

Bet $8 on Red it Loses Balance = $87

Bet $16 on Red it Loses Balance = $71

Bet $32 on Red it Loses Balance = $39

Bet $64 on Red it Loses Balance = $39

Can't place any further bets and there's no manner you'll be able to go back to up to $103 thus you've got lost

This is an example of wishing on an imperfect cash management strategy to win and not relying on a solid system. As a result of quite merely you can't get info or something to offer you a position on variety. If we have a tendency to do flat reckoning on Roulette then the casino edge can slowly diminish our balance conjointly. Quite merely will solely think about luck to create profit here.

If we have a tendency to take the exchange although its parts of foregone conclusion, it isn't mounted odds indulgent, the probabilities of value occupation or out of your favor changes all the time. Affirmative it are often laborious however a decent system will get wise right otherwise there would be no long run profitable traders that I can assure you there are.

Some of the foremost well-known stop loss strategies trailing stop

This is wherever the stop level moves together with the value at a predefined level as set by the merchant. For instance let's say the value is one.22432 and that we wish to sell thus we place our stop at one.22632. Currently if value moves lower to one.22332 then our stop will path behind and move to one.22532 with none input from the merchant. Currently if the value moves against America the stop can stay at one.22532 that in result can defend America from a much bigger loss if we have a tendency to left it at one.22632.

Although this technique will have its pro's and con's.

Pro's = It minimizes losses

Con's = It doesn't permit your trade to breathe and so diminishes some doable smart moves.

But it all depends on the kind of system you utilize. It's immense for if your system predicts breakouts.

Break Even

When value moves in profit by a particular quantity as set by the merchant, the stop loss is affected by the stop loss level to the entry price there by protective the trader from any losses.

For example let's say the value is one.22432 and that we wish to sell thus we place our stop at one.22632. If we expect we must always move stop to interrupt even after we are in profit by twenty pips. Once value reaches one.22232 then the stop is touched from one.22632 to 1.22432 our entry level.

This type of stop loss technique is nice for swing commercialism or once your system plans on holding the trade over daily for a decent trend.

Although this technique will have its pro's and con's.

Pro's = It permits you to carry onto your trade for as long as you're thinking that value can move in your favor.

Con's = as markets do fluctuate it typically will stop you out and then miss out on any profits.

It all depends on however the market behaves and it assume this technique depends on any judgement of the markets behavior.

50% Lock in

This technique involves foremost permitting the trade to breathe and then is suited to holding the trade over daily or a pair of and lockup in half what's there. It's smart as a result of it permits our trade to breathe and is in line with the golden rule of holding on to winners.

It's sensible to enter a purchase order at 8am say the EURUSD at one.22432 with a twenty pip stop loss at one.22232. I return at one2pm to check value is currently at 1.23032 which suggests I'm in profit by sixty pips. Thus I might move my stop to a five hundredth level at one.22732, thus now i do know I've profited despite what however still have an opening of constructing additional profit if value was to maneuver higher.

Stop Reversal

This is after we place associate degree opposite order on a stop loss level. This is often an efficient technique for counteracting once you get the trade wrong. It works so, you'd enter a purchase order on the EURUSD at one.22432 with a twenty pip stop loss at one.22232 however you'd conjointly place associate degree opposite version of that sell order at this stop loss level of one.22232.

Holding over days whereas stopping the most important peaks

With this technique, you may solely be risking twenty pips however each 3-4 trades place can see profits of over one hundred pips as a result of using my favorite is that the five hundredth lock in with a small distinction. Rather than lockup within the five hundredth level I instead look into the previous major value peaks and place my stop at these levels. Value peaks provides a higher plan of true market direction thus what better thanks to hold onto that direction than using price peaks, as though value fluctuates, if it's for instance shorting then value shouldn't rise on top of the previous peaks till there's a significant direction modification.

What is profit issue relation and your ideal risk to reward ratio?

Having seen such a big amount of commercialism systems and that they all look nice on paper however there's one factor they ne'er show and it's all the way down to you to seek out yourself. It's the Profit issue quantitative relation or PFR. This is often wherever you discover the quantitative relation of you profits to your losses. If over several many trades it's still on top of one then your system is profitable. This one major purpose is what all commercialism systems don't really show you, however is what you wish to be a real

Profitable merchant

There was one system remembered particularly that i assume cursed me and is what light-emitting diode me to the goal of holding a trade over many days for max profits whereas risking solely a little quantity. Clearly I can't provide names here however the most promise was most trades build 100+ pips profit by lunch period. Currently like all systems you examine they invariably show you the great whereas glossing over the unhealthy. What they don't show you is that the reality of however that system performs. You'll be able to solely see the truth once you've got bought the system and toughened commercialism it yourself.

So we have a tendency to should back take a look at and notice the systems true PFR.

From expertise my trades sometimes find yourself with a risk reward of one to four which means for each £1 invested with I expect a £4 come for if that trade wins. This statement is inapplicable what extremely matters is that the profit issue quantitative relation. Or just your profits / losses. If it's on top of one then you're in profit. It depends on how high above one on how briskly we will profit and the way a lot of we have a tendency to profit can build. Thus once commercialism I invariably examine my system is functioning and ensuring the PFR is > one.

For example let's say I placed one thousand trades with a strike rate of one in four, and every winning trade to create$20 whereas a losing trade makes $5. We will expect 250 winners and 750 losers. Sounds unhealthy initially, 750 losers Buckeye State No! However watch:

250 winners at $20 a win = $5000

750 losers at $5 a loss = $3750

So,

Profit / Loss = PFR

5000 / 3750 = one.33

Our PFR is one.33 that's i might say a practical PFR. Trading at $1 a pip means that we are going to profit £1250 over one thousand trades placed. $1250 exploit a $100 investment is serious cash creating potential. In fact this is often a conservative PFR there are several systems out there with higher PFR. I've browse that almost all systems realistically reach just below a pair of.0. Mine is 1.33 that is tight enough.

METATRADER SUMMARY STOP LOSS AND TAKE PROFIT

Standard Stop Loss

Stop Loss need to be divided into 2 sorts, same as Take Profit. The primary kind is automatic, the second is manual. The most perform of Stop Loss is to reduce losses once the value rushes in direction that's opposite to the fascinating.

Let's 1st look into the automated Stop Loss. it's activated as follows: an order is opened and value of Stop Loss is being set as an definite quantity under gap value. just in case if the Stop Loss level is reached, the order is closed mechanically.

Let us look into associate degree example.

Ask price=1.4040, Bid=1.4038. We have a tendency to open a purchase order. Gap value is one.4040. Let's set Stop Loss=1.4020. Value ticks down and passes the amount Bid=1.4020. The order is closed mechanically. The loss is twenty pips.

The similar state of affairs for SELL order

Ask price=1.4040, Bid=1.4038. We have a tendency to open a purchase order. Gap value is one.4038. Let's set Stop Loss=1.4063. Value goes upward and passes the amount Ask=1.4063. The order is closed mechanically. The loss is twenty pips.

One of the options of Stop Loss is that it can't be set too getting ready to the order gap value. Lowest distance are often completely different and is being set consistent with configurations of the broker server. Worth is counted from the gap value. I.e. from the raise price for purchase orders and from the terms for SELL orders.

During the time once the order is open, we have a tendency to be ready to modification the Stop Loss worth. Herein, rules for distance of a replacement Stop Loss worth are precisely the same as throughout the order gap. The sole distinction is going to be that current value worth has got to be used however not the order gap price.

For convenience, the traders use relative values of Stop Loss within the pips, e.g., for the worth of SL=25 at current value of Bid=1.4038 and Ask=1.4040, definite quantity of Stop Loss for purchase order are going to be one.4015, and for SELL order below an equivalent conditions it'll be one.4063. I.e., raise price is taken as a basis for the purchase order and terms is taken for the SELL order. Once closing order on Stop Loss event we are going to receive exactly twenty five pips of loss.

Manual Stop Loss.

Manual technique of order closing differs from the automated one within the manner that just in case of reaching Stop Loss level, the order isn't closed mechanically, and it's to be closed manually. Such technique isn't terribly effective as a result of further efforts are needed, however there are cases once it's cheap to use notably manual closing. E.g., after we have to be compelled to use a perform of partial closure of associate degree order below completely different levels of loss for one and also the same order.

Let's take a glance at associate degree example. We have a tendency to open associate degree order with three tons volume. And that we can shut one heap at a unique level of loss. SL1=10, SL2=20, SL3=30. Once reaching SL1 and SL2, components of the order are going to be closed manually and shutting of the half at the SL3 level will be done mechanically.

In this manner, with the terms =1.4038, Ask=1.4040, the parameters:

For purchase order are going to be as follows: open price=1.4040, manual Stop Loss SL1=1.4030, manual Stop Loss=SL2=1.4020, commonplace Stop Loss=SL3=1.4010.

For SELL: open price=1.4008, manual Stop Loss SL1=1.4018, manual Stop Loss=SL2=1.4028, commonplace Stop Loss=SL3=1.4038.

Manual technique of order closing as per the Stop Loss level has one disadvantage minimum. If a technical deficiency suddenly happens on the merchant aspect, then it might be not possible to shut the order timely a minimum of. In automatic technique, order can advance any case in spite of technical state of the metatrader terminal. Thus, merchant is to blame for manual order closing, and broker is to blame for the automated closing. These peculiarities need to be obligatory taken into consideration once selecting parameters for the order being opened.

Standard Take Profit

Two kinds of Take Profit need to be distinguished. The primary kind is automatic, the second is or manual.

Let's look into the automated Take Profit. It's activated as follows: an order is opened and value of Take Profit is being set as a definite quantity on top of gap value. Just in case if the Take Profit level is reached, the order is closed mechanically.

Let us look into associate degree example.

Ask price=1.4040, Bid=1.4038. We have a tendency to open a purchase order. Open value is one.4040. Let's set the Take Profit value=1.4060. The value starts to maneuver up and reaches raise value=1.4060, however the order isn't closed because the purchase order are going to be closed as per the Bid level. The value keeps on growing and passes the Bid level=1.4060. The order is closed mechanically. The profit is twenty pips.

The similar for SELL order. Raise price=1.4040, Bid=1.4038. We have a tendency to open a SELL order. Open value is one.4038. Let's set the Take Profit value=1.4018. Value goes down and passes the raise level=1.4018. The order is closed mechanically. The profit is twenty pips.

One of the options of Take Profit is that it can't be set too getting ready to the order gap value. Lowest distance are often completely different and is being set consistent with configurations of the broker server. Worth is counted from the price. I.e. from the terms for purchase orders and from the raise price for SELL orders.

During the time once the order is open, we have a tendency to be ready to modification the Take Profit worth. Herein, rules for distance of a replacement Take Profit worth are precisely the same as throughout the order gap. The sole distinction are going to be that current value worth has got to be used however not the order open price.

For convenience, the traders use relative values of Take Profit within the pips, e.g., for the worth of TP=25 at current value of Bid=1.4038 and Ask=1.4040, definite quantity of Take Profit for purchase order are going to be one.4065, and for SELL order below an equivalent conditions it'll be - one.4013. I.e., raise price is taken as a basis for the purchase order and terms is taken for the SELL order. During this manner, once closing associate degree order on Take Profit event we are going to receive exactly twenty five pips of profit.

Manual Take Profit.

Manual technique of order closing differs from the automated one within the manner that just in case of reaching Take Profit level, the order isn't closed mechanically, and it's to be closed manually. Such technique isn't terribly effective as a result of further efforts are needed, however there are cases once it's cheap to use notably manual closing. E.g. after we have to be compelled to use a perform of partial closure of associate degree order below completely different levels of profit for one and also the same order.

Let's take a glance at example. We have a tendency to open associate degree order with three tons volume. And that we can shut one heap at a unique level of profit. TP1=10, TP2=20, TP3=30. Once reaching TP1 and TP2 components of the order are going to be closed manually and shutting of the half at the TP3 level will be done mechanically.

With the Ask=1.4040, terms =1.4038 the parameters for purchase order are going to be as follows: open price=1.4040, manual Take Profit TP1=1.4050, manual Take Profit =TP2=1.4060, commonplace Take Profit=TP3=1.4070.

With the Ask=1.4070, terms =1.4068 the parameters for SELL order are going to be as follows: open price=1.4068, manual Take Profit TP1=1.4058, manual Take Profit =TP2=1.4048, commonplace Take Profit=TP3=1.4038.

Manual technique of order closing as per the Take Profit level has one disadvantage minimum. If a technical deficiency suddenly happens on the merchant aspect, then it might be not possible to shut the order timely a minimum of. In automatic technique, order can advance any case in spite of technical state of the metatrader terminal. Thus, the trader is to blame for manual order closing, and broker is to blame for the automated closing. These peculiarities need to be obligatory taken into consideration once selecting parameters for the order being opened.

TRADING WITH STOP LOSS AND TRAILING STOP

There are numerous risk management tools obtainable to the merchant within the exchange (FOREX) market. 2 of the foremost common ones are the stop loss and also the trailing stop. What are they and what are they used for? Are they necessary for victorious trading? This text can assist you to know these ideas and supply answers to those queries.

Stop Loss

The platforms provided by several on-line FOREX brokers contain constitutional options like the stop loss and also the trailing stop to assist manage sure risks inherent in commercialism. A stop loss could be a feature that permits the merchant to pre-determine the value level at which the position are going to be mechanically closed ought to the market move unfavorably against the open position. The first good thing about the stop loss is to place a cap on the number of loss a merchant is willing to suffer. A well-placed stop loss is a necessary element of an efficient trading strategy. There are, however, traders WHO trade while not a stop loss or trade with the stop loss set improperly. Each of those approaches are wooing disasters.

Day traders can generally have a unique approach to setting a stop loss than those that take long positions. As a result of they're additional fascinated by creating fast profits ensuing from tiny market movements, the day traders can generally utilize a smaller stop loss. In distinction, the broader stop is favored by long traders who are less involved with the smaller moves of currency costs, as well as the temporary reversals gift within the trend. Such value reversals would usually trigger the smaller stop loss of the short or day merchant. Positions taken by long traders could also be open for several days or longer, experiencing a good variety of reversals on the thanks to the take-profit target. Consequently, the broader stops would be desirable to the present breed.

Trailing Stop

A trailing stop is usually used in reference to the stop loss. Indeed, it might be futile to try the trailing stop while not 1stsetting the stop loss. That's as a result of the most purpose of the trailing stop is to maneuver the stop loss incrementally within the direction of the profit target because the currency value moves manner. Such has the result of incrementally cloth profits whereas the position remains open. The first stop loss level can't be reached by the value reversal while not the trader's position having first been closed mechanically at the new stop loss level created do able by the trailing stop.

In a news commercialism situation--generally characterized by speedy value movement--a merchant would ideally utilize the tiniest progressive trailing stop allowed. The smaller the trailing stop, the additional chance there's for creating and keeping pips while not being subjected to the vagaries of whipsaws or different speedy reversals in currency value. As within the case of the stop loss itself, a smaller trailing stop would be favored by the short merchant. for instance, rather than looking forward to the value to maneuver twenty pips before the stop loss is touched and also the 20-pip profit complete, the merchant will understand profits earlier by setting the trailing stop at ten pips, with the expectation of cloth ten pips with every 10-pip move within the currency value. Though it might be a trader's dream to own a trailing stop as low as one or five, the bottom to be found on any broker's platform is perhaps ten. Still, by utilizing a well-place stop loss with the acceptable trailing stop, a merchant will invest fruitfully and minimize the inevitable risks whereas conserving precious commercialism capital.

SEVEN COMMON STOP LOSS EXITS

A stop loss order can mechanically shut a trade at a group level so as to forestall any losses. If a purchase order has been placed, then the stop level is ready at a value that's under the shopping for price. On the opposite hand, if a sell order was triggered, then the stop are going to be placed on top of the terms.

A general rule is that the exit strategy should coordinate with a trader's entries and his overall commercialism system. For trending system, it's needed that the merchant set a much bigger stop loss level that permits additional area for the trade to breathe. If it's an investor system or flight system, a little stop loss ought to be set so trade can exit like a shot if it's a nasty trade. Thereby, traders' loss are going to be restricted in such forex commercialism system.

There are a range of stops that one will incorporate into a system.

1. Initial Stop

This is the primary stop set at the start of the trade. This stop is known before getting into the market. It's accustomed calculate the position size of the position at that to trade and this is often conjointly the most important loss a merchant can absorb this trade.

2. Trailing Stop

Develops because the market moves. This stop allows the merchant to lock in profit because the market moves within the favor. Trailing stop ensures that the stop loss follows the value movements closely because the trend develops. This is often to forestall any unexpected market movements from taking away profits ought to the trend starts to reverse.

3. 2 Bar Trailing Stop

This is employed in a trend if the market looks to be losing momentum and a reversal is anticipated.

4. Moving Average Trailing Stop

Moving average indicator is commonest used for trailing stop loss.

5. Average True vary Trailing Stop

Also referred to as ATR indicator. This indicator is generally utilized by turtle traders or trend following traders to see market volatility and place their stop loss removed from volatility and protective their profits at an equivalent time.

6. Parabolic SAR Trailing Stop

Another indicator wide used for putting your stop loss.

7. Channel Trailing Stop

An unremarkably used trailing stop technique for turtle traders or trend following traders.

Is Your Stop-Loss choice supported Market Dynamics?

It implies that have you ever taken in to account market conditions which will tell you the way a lot of area you wish to offer the trade to breathe so your trade won't be exited thanks to market noises and repeatedly stop out? There's no excellent stop-loss strategy however the foremost ideal stop loss strategy has got to be discovered and puzzled out by the merchant via back testing and forward testing.

Forex Trailer could be a totally freelance computer code Semitic deity that manages traders' positions within the exchange market. Forex Trailer ensures they're closely monitored to shut for optimum profits. It works by managing the merchant's stop loss level or take profit levels and thereby lockup in profits for the trader.

FUNDAMENTAL VS TECHNICAL ANALYSIS

Investors use variety of techniques to gauge stocks before creating a trade or long investment call. The 2 core techniques used will loosely be divided into elementary analysis and technical analysis. Each ways use completely different methodologies to do to predict movements within the market, and each are often quite valuable for serving to investors to create selections.

What is Fundamental Analysis?

Fundamental analysis focuses on a company's monetary and market position, growth prospects, and monetary performance. The construct considers all the economic factors concerned in equity valuation. It's at each monetary statements and also the company's market position and the political or economic climate to assist investors build long selections. Usually, stocks are bought once a value falls below the share's calculable intrinsic worth, and so it's command for an extended time. Elementary analysis tends to maneuver a bit additional slowly and concentrates on a company's monetary indicators and may utilize relative valuation like Price/Earnings quantitative relation (PE ratio) and/or absolute valuation such as free income. It's priceless for somebody who is searching for a longer-term investment and isn't troubled most concerning short market movements. Elementary analysis works in accordance with the finance technique of getting a margin of safety. The concept is to shop for a stock once its value quite its value on the marketplace for elementary analysis, for instance, you may return up with associate degree intrinsic worth of one hundred. That doesn't mean you'd purchase the stock at ninety eight or ninety nine. If you've got determined to use a margin of safety of 15 August

1945, you'd solely purchase the stock at eighty five or below. Elementary analysis works off 2 central assumptions:

• the worth} of a given stock can eventually correct to its intrinsic value.

• shopping for associate degree undervalued stock and holding it for long enough ought to earn returns because the share value converges to its intrinsic worth.

Hence, why elementary analysis is popular investors WHO use the purchase and hold worth philosophy.

What Is Technical Analysis?

Technical analysis could be an additional short approach to finance. The construct analyzes charts, past stock valuation and volume knowledge, and examines historical knowledge to seek out patterns in an endeavor to predict future trends. It's the analysis of a company's technical indicators like value movements and commercialism volume metrics, a business's strength relative to its peers within the same sector/overall market, and different similar indices. Technical analysis is employed for short commercialism instead of long finance and applies ideas like the Dow Theory and trend following to see what to shop for and sell. In technical analysis, there are 3 golden rules consistent with agreement within the market: Rule 1: Stock costs mirror everything that has and may have an effect on a corporation. All the knowledge associate degree capitalist desires is mirrored within the market value. Rule 2: Movements in valuation don't seem to be random. Stock costs move in trends, don't fight them. Rule 3: value patterns invariably repeat—given enough time. The repetitive nature of value movements is all the way down to market psychology: Investors are consistent in their reactions.

Investing vs. Trading

Many people grow their money within the stock market—otherwise, it wouldn't be as standard because it is! Some build cash by commercialism, and a few by finance. Warren Buffett, for instance, is associate degree finance icon notable for creating billions due to long strategic investments. Buffett buys firms and holds onto their stock, typically for many years. He believes in taking a slow, steady long read. He even buys once others are too fearful e.g., in market downturns (assuming that his elementary analysis advised the acquisition makes sense) and he with patience waits for the proper time to sell. Buffett's wealth building strategy works in sharp distinction to legendary hedge-fund manager St. GeorgeSoros, WHO has conjointly created billions however through commercialism and technical analysis. Soros has created many fortunes by taking advantage of the constant state of flux within the markets.

Valuing Assets

If you're a novice or long capitalist, then it's a decent plan to specialize in fundamentals 1st. Investors that have an interest in growth and worth ought to contemplate whether or not this value of a stock is sensible once examining the health and prospects of the corporate that they're evaluating. Growth investors place loads of stress on whether or not a corporation goes to be ready to thrive and grow. it's common for businesses to struggle in its time period, however if a corporation that's not profitable too soon remains ready to show growth in revenue, then which will typically be enough to draw in investors WHO believe that substantial profits are on the horizon long. Those investors could hope to check a situation wherever the corporate breaks through those development stages and thrives to become massively profitable. Growth investors could also be willing to carry for an extended time, and in and of itself elementary analysis be for them. Fundamentals are prestigious for worth investors too, however the prevailing market condition will play a major role. The stock in question ought to be obtainable within the market at an affordable value (i.e., its letter of the alphabet quantitative relation and also the price-to-book worth ought to be favorable). Worth finance is concerning shopping for stocks once they're undervalued (to the estimate of the true/intrinsic value) and employing a margin of safety to it value. Worth investors have an interest within the past and current performance of a stock, and whether or not the basics are sound. Once investors have found stocks that look appealing, technical analysis will facilitate them to make your mind up if the short trades being thought of can compute in their favor. Technical analysis includes stock screening, charting, and examines moving averages and random oscillators to offer a plan of wherever a value is relative to its price vary over a selected amount. If a stock is commercialism in a very vary that shows that the stochastics have touched into 'overbought' or 'oversold', then it are often seen as an indication of a possible value reversal on the horizon. Several investors use these as market signals for once to create trades.

When to Use every Technique

Use elementary analysis if you've got an extended investment horizon and you wish to see the intrinsic worth of a stock. Use technical analysis for short market selections once you wish to make your mind up whether or not this is often the proper time to shop for or sell a foothold supported each current and past trends.

Both Techniques Have worth

if you're a short merchant, then technical analysis, combined with stop losses and take profit orders will assist you build hip selections. If you're a long capitalist, then basing your selections on fundamentals, and ignoring short blips that drive those technical trades ought to serve you well. Stock choice doesn't need to be a parcel of land, however it's crucial to be versatile and broad-minded. Avoid changing into showing emotion connected to anyone stock or sector. Base your equity valuations on data and logic, instead of gut feeling, and take a look at to remain disciplined. Even the most effective traders build unhealthy trades, however those trades don't need to result in disaster if you manage the chance in your portfolio and bankroll well.

COMBINING TECHNICAL AND FUNDAMENTAL ANALYSIS

Technical analysis could be a sturdy instrument within the trader's outfit and, in fact, several investors argue that it's the foremost vital style of analysis. All the same, once one tool has such a fabric impact on your decision making process its value appreciating its assumptions and potential limitations.

Stock Market Models

the validity of technical analysis relies on behavioural finance that studies however social, psychological feature and emotional biases have an effect on the value movements of the stock markets.

The two main observations from behavioral finance are:

1) Investors tend to create systematic errors that have an effect on the market and deduct the benefits of market potency

2) Traders will fail to come about a loss and, though all indicators show that the market can still trend against them, they create the irrational call to carry their position and thence incur even bigger losses

A different model for exchange movement is that the 'Efficient Market Hypothesis' (EMH) that states that the value of a stock at any given moment represents a rational analysis of all the notable info.

The EMH model has a minimum of 2 attention-grabbing consequences:

1) The return on equity are often expected to be slightly bigger than that obtainable from non-equity investments. If this wasn't the case

then an equivalent rational calculations would lead equity investors to shift their funds to those safer non-equity investments that would be expected to offer the same or higher come at a lower risk level

2) as a result of the value of a share at each given moment is an 'efficient' reflection of mean value the curve of expected come costs can tend to follow a 'random walk'. This can be determined by the random emergence of data over time

Combining Technical and elementary Analysis

So, how will such models be employed in order to create additional hip commercialism decisions?

When stepping into a foothold it's vital to know the market paradigm at the time of the choice with relevancy the foremost relevant economic indicators. For instance, if associate degree capitalist is commercialism the GBP/USD unfold indulgent market then they must record this state of affairs and expectations for each economies.

Below is associate degree example of however a capitalist may mix technical and elementary analysis once considering a foothold on the GBP/USD market. during this case the capitalist is creating use of a daily chart:

Technical Summary:

— GBP has been gaining against the USD since could of this year and is supported by a firm rising line

— The twenty days EMA is on top of the fifty days EMA that supports the optimistic read

– MACD (12,26,9) is on top of zero and looks to be consolidating with its signal line which can be simply another corrective movement in a very market

– RSI (14) is neutral

– random (28,6,6) is showing signs of optimistic divergence

– Summary: The capitalist might conceive to go long on top of $1.595 with targets of $1.63 and $1.65

Fundamental Summary:

Lagging Indicators Recent unleashs agreement For Next unleash Recent Releases agreement For Next Release

Employment nine.7%, 9.6% (MOM) 9.6% 7.6% 7.6%

Overnight Interest Rates one.0% 1.0% 0.5% 0.5%

GDP 1.8%, 2.0% 2.1% 1.2%, 0.8% (QOQ) 0.8%

CPI 1.0%,1.1% 1.0% 0.5%, 0.0% (MOM) 0.2%

The on top of table/fundamental outline is simply a look at a number of the most figures, there are different key indicators that would be enclosed like funds, client sentiment and building permits. It's conjointly vital to require into consideration the general commercial enterprise and financial policy of the central banks and governments concerned.

If we have a tendency to attempt to summarize each sorts of analysis, we will observe a consolidating optimistic trend combined with a divergence in financial policies wherever the America is increasing and UK is pushing for non indulgence.

So, associate degree capitalist could conceive to take an optimistic read on the GBP/USD market and be careful for any changes within the current market paradigm. As long because the new info is in line with agreement, it would be expected that the technical trend can still be sustained. Any new info that challenges current expectations might manifest in associate degree adverse reaction on the currency combine.

The on top of regime could sound like effortful work, however, in my expertise, most retail traders don't appear to own the discipline to follow such analysis. On the opposite hand, it's a notable indisputable fact that most retail traders are internet losers thus it would be value setting up the additional effort.

Spread indulgent carries a high level of risk and you'll be able to lose quite your initial deposit, thus you must guarantee unfold indulgent meets your investment objectives.

WHY TO IGNORE FUNDAMENTALS THROUGHOUT DAY TRADING

Whether you day trade Forex, stocks or futures, don't get distracted by elementary analysis. Whereas fundamentals are relevant to long investors, day traders can doubtless notice that elementary analysis doesn't improve their performance on short trades. Most victorious day trades don't concern themselves with fundamentals. Here's why.

Fundamental Analysis Is inapplicable on Short Time Frames

For a trade that last 5 minutes, what's on a company's record isn't about to matter a lot of. A corporation will have atrocious monetary statements, and however for months on finish, it will rally. A corporation are often sturdy financially, with nice earnings, and however some days the share value can drop sort of a rock. The purpose is, fundamentals don't matter on short trades.

Anything will happen inside the terribly short time length of daily trade as a result of the value is usually moving, each up and down. As day traders we have a tendency to don't have to be compelled to understand something concerning the financials of the corporate we are commercialism. Such knowledge can solely serve to distract America. If you realize the monetary position of a corporation, don't let it bias your trades. As indicated, something will happen throughout someday, and particularly throughout one trade.

Day commercialism Profits Don't think about elementary Analysis

As daily merchant, the first goal is to systematically implement a commercialism arrange. Researching however unhealthy or smart a corporation is doing only blinds us to what's happening on the sole real piece of timely info that matters--the value chart of that company (or forex combine or futures contract).

The price chart tells America precisely what associate degree plus is doing at any given time. By analyzing the value chart we will notice trade setups supported our commercialism arrange. If a commercialism arrange or strategy has been tried profitable, then there's no would like for fundamentals. Day traders are more contented commercialism and formulating ways supported continuance value (chart) patterns that occur on a daily basis and going away the elemental trades to long investors (who aren't troubled concerning minor intraday price fluctuations).

TRADING PSYCHOLOGY

Once you mastered the science of trading you're able to win. One among the explanations that commercialism is thus difficult is as a result of it pulls on your emotions. When you are in a very trade and you see value move against you the natural reaction is to feel worry. Once you see value move in your favor and you create cash you hope for additional, this is often greed. It's not wrong to own these emotions. It's utterly natural.

Fight or flight response

Human beings are programmed to react to emotions, positive and negative. The human brain has in-built protection mechanisms that stimulate behavioral responses. Typically after we feel worry we respond by using our fight or flight mechanism. Back within the day after we were living amongst wild animals this was a helpful response. It might save our lives! In most areas of life this fight or flight reaction remains helpful. If we have a tendency to are in peril, then we feel worry and that we have to be compelled to take action. We have a tendency to either have to be compelled to get the euphemism out of there or resolve to fight our reply of matters if we decide this to be doable.

Fear in trading

Trading stimulates this in-built fight or flight mechanism. A trade that we have a tendency to are in goes against America. We have a tendency to worry losing cash. Our brain responds to the present worry by triggering automatic action. While not totally considering what's happening we have a tendency to exit trades to chop our losses. This is often our solely choice within the immediate moment.

We have a tendency to can't move value action on our own, thus fighting our reply isn't a doable different.

Once we've got exited a trade for a loss the worry is replaced by different negative emotions, frustration, guilt, anger, regret. We have a tendency to then do have associate degree choice to fight, we will enter another trade. Red mist descends. After we enter trades doltishly we don't seem to be following our system and this is often terribly dangerous. It will result in serious losses.

The moment that we have a tendency to enter a trade our minds are like a shot altered whether or not we adore it or not. Our thoughts are clouded by the commitment that we've got created, the judgement that we've got created. We glance for reasons to prove that we have a tendency to be right. We have a tendency to hope to create cash. This is often referred to as the confirmation bias. It's supported eager to be tested right, worry of being wrong and greed. Yes, sorry it's greed.

For these reasons commercialism is extremely difficult.

Reactions to our emotions within the style of the fight or flight response are the explanation why we have a tendency to exit trades at the worst doable time and enter trades at the worst possible time. They're the explanation that we have a tendency to don't follow our system and that they are the reason why we will have an awfully profitable system on paper however still lose cash.

Master the science of trading

Let ME offer you some samples of how science in commercialism works:

You enter a trade supported your system providing you with a sign to shop for.

Scenario 1

Price goes up. You're earning money.

Some commercialism portals show you the way a lot of cash that you just are presently up or down on every trade and as value moves thus will this figure. This is often not helpful.

You see that you just have created cash. What will your mind then do? It says to you, "Exit now and take your cash." This is often due to worry of losing what you've got. If you focus on this thought for too long then you'll exit your position.

If you ignore the thought then as presently as value goes down slightly the thought are going to be back, even stronger now, you'll exit your position.

If you ignore the thought and value rises then the thought can come, once more it'll be even stronger currently. "Take your cash whereas you'll be able to. Costs invariably go down once they need gone up!" you'll exit your position.

This is the explanation why it's difficult to run our profitable trades and also the reason why we regularly exit profitable trades at the worst time, at the top of pullbacks and simply before value zooms off within the direction that we have a tendency to think that it might go.

Scenario 2

Price goes down. Not what you were expecting. You're losing cash. You seek for reasons why it went down hoping to seek out them and see value rising back to your entry level. You explore for indications that costs can rise. You ignore indications that it'll continue falling.

Before you recognize it you're in a very losing trade. You resort to hope. You hope that costs can rise. Thoughts like "if it simply goes back to wherever I entered i will be able to get out" enter your head.

Eventually value falls any and continues falling. You exit your position, feeling desperate.

This is the explanation why it's simple to ignore once you are wrong and cut your losses and also the reason why we regularly exit losing trades at the worst doable time, even as value reaches the acute within the other way to our trade and turns back towards our entry purpose.

Trade your system and ignore the cash

- All traders ought to have smart reasons to enter trades. The explanations ought to be supported by a system that has tested profitable over an extended amount of your time in back testing.

- All trades ought to have target levels and criteria for exiting at a profit if this target isn't met.

- All trades ought to have specific criteria that tell you that you just are wrong.

- All trades ought to have a physical stop level to confirm that if one thing goes seriously wrong you don't lose your house! The particular stop level determined to by your system could or might not be an equivalent level as your physical stop.

- You must solely exit trades supported the standards determined to by your system.

Mental and physical stop positions ought to be evaluated before getting into a trade. If the amount at that you'd be wrong implies that you would lose an excessive amount of cash for you then don't enter the trade.

If you enter trades thinking one thing like "I'll simply see however it goes" then you'll suffer from emotional commercialism. Little question concerning it.

Assuming that you just have entered a trade supported the foundations of your system then you must see the trade through and ignore the cash. You're getting into trades supported a tested system and through the trade isn't the time to start out re-evaluating the chances of a system operating or not.

If you're unsure of the effectiveness of your system then you wish to try and do additional analysis in back testing it.

Trades that begin badly

Sometimes winning trades do begin badly. This doesn't essentially mean that it's about to be a losing trade.

Beginning traders must always trade with the trend. The explanation is as a result of the trend indicates the final direction of the market.

If you enter a trade supported a trend based mostly system and you're commercialism with the trend then bear in mind that trends do have pullbacks and pullbacks can feel painful.

In a pullback once value action appearance at its worst for you then this is often most likely the worst time to exit. in a very trend once value pulls back powerfully then the probabilities are that if the trend continues it'll rebound strongly too. Hold on till your exit criteria has been met.

Most sturdy value moves conjointly rebound powerfully. If you're watching holders on your chart and you get a negative candlestick within the other way to the trend then it's typically followed by an awfully sturdy candlestick or series of candlesticks back in the direction of the trend. the difficulty is that once all you'll be able to see is value action going against you and your open position going negative you'll become fearful and it'll go away your fight or flight mechanism. Watch for your exit criteria to be met before exiting.

When value goes in your favor then hang on in there. Once value moves powerfully in your favor you'll desire exiting the trade. You recognize that value is probably going to pullback at some stage this is often about to cause you to nervous unless you settle for that this is the case and see the larger image. Once you see the pullback happening then you'll desire exiting the trade as you'll be able to see your profits evaporating. You'll be sorry that you just didn't take profits earlier. Suspend on in there. See the trade through. Watch for value to create your target or trigger associate degree exit via your exit criteria.

Always bear in mind that commercialism is least profitable within the long-term once you answer spikes in value action (with you and against you) and exit before your system criteria are met. Settle for that typically trades fail. No system is 100 percent effective. Settle for that typically you'll build losses. Losses are a suitable a part of a winning and profitable system. Invariably trade your system.

Trades that go against you – Knowing once you are wrong

I can't emphasize enough the necessity to stay to a system in commercialism. Bear in mind that commercialism could be a terribly competitive world. Individual traders (lone traders) such as you and that i are battling against a number of the richest individuals and organizations within the world. These massive players all have systems. Several of those systems are devised over time by the some of the brightest individuals on the world. Cash can purchase you the absolute best of everything.

Having aforementioned that, commercialism is truly really easy. Once value goes up and also the action meets the standards of your commercialism system, buy. Once value fall, sell. If we have a tendency to try this then we will build cash. Lots of it.

When I mention massive players. I'm talking a few variety of massive players with variant cash. All of them understand the foundations of the sport and it's a game once all!

The big players within the markets have systems that incorporate what time has told America concerning science. it's all concerning smoke and mirrors at a fancy level. Massive players understand that almost all inexperienced and amateur traders can sponsor the topnotch and sell at the bottoms. Once things look nice then be terribly skeptical!

The big players understand that once amateurs sponsor topnotch they're going to be fearful if costs move against them. They understand wherever amateurs are doubtless to put their stops.

Their job is to require simple cash from beginners and amateurs. As a result of they savvy the sport operates they're going to deliberately trade against smaller traders. They're going to deliberately move value within the short term in the other way to wherever they will send it in the long run. In doing this they're going to sell at topnotch and sponsor bottoms. They wipe out smaller traders' stops, so providing themselves with excellent worth contracts before taking he market within the different direction.

Smoke and Mirrors

Just before a market makes an enormous shift, more often than not, the value action can build a fast move that hints at a move within the other way to wherever it's about to go. This is often smoke and mirrors. It's sort of a nutmeg in soccer (sending the ball between associate degree opponent's legs). It's sort of a server in court game feigning to send to ball in one direction before causation it within the different.

This fast move can attract amateur traders. they're going to trade the direction that they see the market moving towards a flight, this is often once the market appearance nice, but it's conjointly once there's the foremost danger. The massive players will move the market several times in several directions terribly quickly before the big move is confirmed. When the market feigns a flight amateur traders jump aboard and so get worn out.

Example:

Price can build steady progress upwards, moving to the highest of a variety. Amateurs are going to be thinking "Price goes up." Then value dives down all of an unexpected. The amateurs then assume "Oh, value goes down. Look into that!" they're going to exit long positions and enter short positions. Value can then move upwards powerfully, breaking the previous highs and zooming for the sky. In fact this can do away with all of the amateur traders' stops on their shorts, so fast the move upwards and providing low-cost and simply come-at-able contracts for the professionals.

These sort of moves happen all the time and also the amateur traders will build many losing trades in a very row chasing the market up and down during this manner. By the time the market makes its massive move the amateur has been agitated out, and usually sits in their chair, confounded by their losses, looking at the market zooming away while not them.

This is how markets operate. This is often the sport. As you learn to trade you wish to bear in mind of however this works, however the science of it works and you wish to own a commercialism system that enables for this and embraces this.

It is an enormous game. a awfully vital game. As a lone merchant we have a tendency to be on the skin wanting in. It isn't our game, it belongs to the massive players. The massive players permit America into the sport, indeed they encourage America to play as they understand that we offer simple cash for them.

It is a game the lone merchant will win as long as we have a tendency to play it by their rules.

SIX sensible TIPS TO MASTER MIND AND cash

You know this:

Cut your losses and ride your profits.

But once the time comes, you are doing the precise opposite!

Why?

Because of your commercialism science.

When you're presupposed to cut your losses, you hold onto your losses… hoping it turns around thus you don't suffer a loss.

When you're presupposed to ride your profits, you exit your winners… fearing that it would turn out to be losses.

Weird right?

And this is often simply the tip of the iceberg.

I get it. I've been there myself. i do know what you're browsing.

So in today's commercialism science post, you'll learn six insanely sensible tips to master your mind and cash.

I'm not about to provide mumbo elephantine recommendation and tell you to be an additional disciplined merchant. You recognize that already.

Instead, the question is… how?

Then let's begin…

Get employment and overcome most of your commercialism science problems instantly

I know this might sound weird…

…but being employed (or alternate supply of income) improves your commercialism science and results.

Here's why:

- It removes the necessity to create cash syndrome
- It allows you to grow your commercialism account quickly

Let ME explain…

It removes the necessity to create cash syndrome

Here's the thing:

If commercialism is your solely supply of financial gain, you're golf shot yourself at an obstacle psychologically.

Why?

Because you'll have the necessity to create cash monthly.

This cause you to create poor commercialism selections like widening your stop loss, averaging into losers, commercialism large, and etc.

And that's why several skilled traders don't think about commercialism as their solely supply of financial gain.

Don't believe ME? Let me prove it to you…

Ed Seykota, a Market Wizard, features a trading tribe that price $99/month.

Mark Minervini, a exchange Wizard, offers a master merchant program that price $5000.

Most hedge funds (even the most effective ones) charge a management fee per annum —even if it's a losing year.

To put things in perspective, if you run a billion dollar hedge fund and take a a pair of management fee, it means that you get $20m a year — secured.

As you'll be able to see, skilled traders and hedge funds structure their commercialism in a very manner that it's not their solely supply of financial gain.

So what will a retail merchant such as you do, if you wish to level the taking part in field?

Simple — get employment.

Let ME explain…

If you've got employment, you've got a supply of financial gain monthly despite what. this enables you to specialize in your commercialism while not having to stress whether or not you'll be able to pay the bills this month, or not.

And that's not all because…

It allows you to grow your account faster thus you'll be able to trade larger and build extra money

Here's the thing:

You need cash to create money in commercialism.

Let's say your average come is concerning two hundredth a year. This means…

On a $1000 account, you'll build concerning $200 p.a..

On a $100,000 account, you'll build concerning $20,000 p.a..

On a $1m account, you'll build concerning $200,000 p.a..

So currently the question is…

…how does one increase the scale of your commercialism account?

Well, you'll be able to use a little of your financial gain (from your job) to extend the scale of your trading account. This implies you'll be able to trade larger and build extra money.

And in my opinion, this is one among the most effective belongings you can do for your commercialism — having a regular job.

Back take a look at your strategy and gain huge confidence in your commercialism

Here's the thing:

One of the most important struggles you'll face has the arrogance in your commercialism strategy.

Think about it…

If your commercialism strategy doesn't have a position within the markets, however does one notice the conviction to trade it throughout a drawdown?

You won't.

And instead, you'll begin searching for consequent "best" commercialism strategy — and also the cycle rinse repeats itself.

So here's the deal:

To break out of the cycle, you need to have a position within the markets thus you've got conviction in your commercialism strategy.

So, however are you able to act it?

Back testing.

This refers to however your commercialism strategy works with past knowledge to make your mind up if it's a position within the markets.

Now, if your commercialism strategy is tried to figure using past knowledge, then there's a decent probability it'll add the longer term — which supplies you confidence in your commercialism, right?

So, here are a pair of ways that you'll be able to do it:

1. Manual back testing

2. Systematic back testing

RISK MANAGEMENT

It's not uncommon for beginner Forex traders to assume that creating cash through on-line Forex commercialism is quick and straightforward.

However, it's a method that takes time, dedication, commitment, and patience, if you wish to achieve success and profitable within the Forex market in the long-term.

You can't simply open a foothold in your commercialism platform while not taking into consideration the trading conditions set by your Forex broker, the currency risk, and also the commercialism risk which will have an effect on your invested with capital.

You also have to be compelled to apply tools and techniques to manage your cash and risks – if you don't do those things, you wouldn't be commercialism – you'd be gambling.

Check out these forex risk management tips.

#1 solely INVEST cash YOU DON'T would like

It might sound obvious, however the primary rule in currency trading is to solely risk the cash you'll be able to afford to lose. Several traders, particularly beginners, skip this rule as a result of they assume that it "won't happen to them".

If commercialism were like gambling at a casino, you wouldn't take all the cash you've got to the casino to play black, right? Well, it's an equivalent with commercialism – don't take gratuitous risks by using cash you wish to measure.

Why?

Because it's possible to lose all of your commercialism capital, and second, as a result of commercialism with funds you reside on can add further pressure and emotional stress to your trading, compromising your higher cognitive process abilities and increasing the probabilities of constructing mistakes.

The exchange market could be a terribly volatile and unpredictable market, thus it's better to trade "conservative amounts" from your income.

#2 suppose YOUR RISK TOLERANCE

Before you begin commercialism, you wish to see your risk tolerance, relying on:

- Your age
- Your data of FX commercialism
- Your expertise
- what quantity you're willing to lose
- And your investment goals

Knowing your risk tolerance isn't close to serving to you sleep higher at the hours of darkness, or stress less concerning currency fluctuations.

It's concerning knowing you're on top of things of matters, as a result of your finance the proper quantity of cash vis-à-vis your personal monetary state of affairs in relevancy your financial objectives.

Keep your finance inside your risk tolerance and you decrease the chance of commercialism ruin.

#3 SET YOUR RISK/REWARD quantitative relation TO A MINIMUM OF 1:3

Knowing concerning risk/reward quantitative relation (RRR) will certainly improve your possibilities of changing into profitable within the long-term, setting limit orders (stop-loss and take-profit) that defend your capital.

A RRR measures and compares the space between your entry purpose and your stop-loss and take-profit orders.

For example

Let's say that you're finance on the EUR/USD.

If the space between your entry level and your stop-loss is fifty pips, and also the distance between your entry purpose and your take-profit is a hundred and fifty pips, then you'd be employing a RRR of 1:3, as a result of you're risking fifty pips to earn a hundred and fifty pips (150/50 = 3).

The risk/reward quantitative relation could be a necessary tool to line your stop-loss and take-profit orders counting on your risk tolerance, and each wise merchant ought to management the draw back risk.

Even though crucial a RRR depends on every trader's risk tolerance, it's common to use a risk/reward quantitative relation of 1:3, wherever you expect to earn three times what you're willing to lose.

4# management YOUR RISK PER TRADE

When wondering risks, you furthermore may have to be compelled to contemplate your commercialism capital.

You should solely invest a little portion of your commercialism capital per trade: a decent start line would be to not invest quite a pair of of your obtainable capital per trade.

Expert tip

If you've got $10,000 in your Forex commercialism account, the most loss allowable would be $200 per trade.

Determining the chance per trade could be a useful tool if you bear a run, thus then you'll be able to higher defend your commercialism capital, and avoid giant drawdowns in your commercialism account.

#5 KEEP YOUR RISK CONSISTENT

Most beginners can increase the scale of their positions as presently as they're creating profits, that is one among the most effective ways that to induce your account worn out. Keep your risk consistent!

Do not become over-confident and fewer risk-averse

Just because you've created many winning trades doesn't mean that consequent one goes to be profitable.

Do not become over-confident and fewer risk-averse, as which will result in you ever-changing your cash and risk management rules while not solid reasons.

When you worked on your trade arrange, you had to line up rules to make your mind up concerning an efficient size for your positions. This is often only 1 step in establishing a victorious trading technique, currently you wish to stay to and follow your investment plan!

#6 perceive AND management LEVERAGE

The Forex market could be a leveraged market, owing to its high liquidity.

Leverage implies that you'll be able to invest extra money than your initial deposit, due to margin commercialism. Your broker can solely raise you to place aside a little portion of the full worth of the position you wish to open as collateral.

When using leverage, your profits are often enlarged quickly, however keep in mind that an equivalent applies to your losses. This is often why you wish to know however leverage and margin commercialism work, yet as however they impact your overall performance and commercialism.

Forex traders are typically tempted to use high leverage to create vital profits, however if you're over-leveraged one fast modification within the market might simply wipe you out.

To note

In August 2018, the ecu Securities and Markets Authority (ESMA) obligatory limitations on the leverage offered by brokers. These leverage limits on the gap positions by retail investors vary counting on the underlying:

• 30:1 for major currency pairs

• and 20:1 for non-major currency pairs

#7 TAKE CURRENCY CORRELATIONS INTO thought

Because currencies are priced in pairs, it's vital to know that currencies are connected to every different, or related .

Knowing concerning Forex correlations can assist you higher management your Forex portfolio's exposure by reducing the general risks.

To use FX correlations to your advantage, you wish to recollect many things:

Avoid gap many positions that eliminate one another

For instance, if you go long on the EUR/USD and also the USD/CHF, you'll be able to expect each currency pairs to evolve in opposite directions, that is nearly like having no commercialism position in your account.

Why?

Because the USD is employed once as a base currency (USD/CHF), and once because the quote currency (EUR/USD), which suggests that if the USD strengthens against its major counterparts, then the EUR/USD can go down, whereas the USD/CHD can go up – the evolution of 1 rate cancelling out the opposite one.

Avoid gap positions with an equivalent base currency, or quote currency

For instance, if you go long on the EUR/USD, the AUD/USD, and also the GBP/USD, you'll be able to expect these currency pairs to be completely related as a result of all of them having an equivalent quote currency, the USD.

It implies that once the USD strengthens/weakens, your portfolio can go up/down.

Be aware of goods currencies

Commodity currencies represent currencies that move in accordance with goods costs, as a result of the countries they represent are heavily-dependent on the export of those commodities.

As a general rule, if the value of commodities strengthen, then the currencies of the goods producers can go up – and vice-versa.

The main correlations to grasp concerning are the Canadian dollar (CAD) and oil, the dollar (AUD) and gold/iron core, yet because the New-Zealand dollar (NZD) and wool and farm product.

To improve your Forex commercialism performance, you must perceive your exposure: some currency pairs move along, whereas others evolve in opposite directions. The secret's to diversify your portfolio to mitigate risks.

These tips are simply the cornerstone to higher manage your risk – as you analysis any, you'll notice different Forex commercialism tools and techniques for beginners you'll be able to use to boost your trading strategy.

Before employing a live commercialism account, attempt to back-test your commercialism arrange on a demo account, and improve your strategy if required.

HOW MUCH DO I want TO TRADE FOREX

How Much cash Do I want to Trade Forex?

How much cash you'll have to be compelled to trade forex is one among the primary problems you've got to handle if you wish to become a forex merchant. That broker you select, commercialism platform or strategy you use are all vital yet, however what quantity cash you begin with are going to be a huge determinant in your final success.

Not all traders are alike although, and not everybody trades an equivalent manner. Daily merchant might not would like an equivalent quantity of cash to start out forex commercialism as a swing trader will. The number of cash you wish to trade forex will be determined by your goals. Are you wanting to easily grow your account, or does one ask for regular financial gain from your forex trading?

Below, we are going to look into the advocate capital needed for numerous forex commercialism designs.

How Much cash do I want to Trade Forex? – Why It Matters

Before going into what amount of cash you'll have to be compelled to trade forex effectively, we want to appear at why this issue is even vital. Will it extremely matter if you begin associate degree account with $100 or $3000? Yes!

One of the foremost vital problems new traders face is being under-capitalized. Forex brokers are guilty of fostering such associate degree surroundings by giving to open accounts for as very little as $5 in some cases...although the minimum gap balance is sometimes concerning $100. Let's face it, if you wish to start out commercialism, it's doubtless as a result of you wish associate degree financial gain stream. Well, you aren't about to have a lot of of associate degree financial gain stream if you begin with $100. Since only a few individuals are patient enough to let their account grow, they're going to risk manner an excessive amount of of their capital on every trade attempting to create a financial gain, and within the method lose everything.

I am a firm believer in precisely risking 1 Chronicles of capital (max 3%) on one trade. If your account is $100 meaning you'll be able to solely risk $1 per trade. within the forex market meaning you'll be able to take a 1 small heap position (see hard Pip worth for info on numerous lot sizes), wherever every pip movement is value concerning ten cents, and you wish to stay the chance to but ten pips. Trading during this manner, if you've got a decent strategy, you'll average a few bucks profit daily. whereas this can build your account slowly, most traders don't wish to create a few bucks daily, they require to create their account a lot of quicker and so can risk $10 or $20 per trade—sometimes more—in an endeavor to show that $100 into thousands as quickly as doable. This might work for a time, however sometimes leads to associate degree account balance of $0.

The other downside with Forex trading with such a little amount of cash is that it offers nearly no flexibility within the form of trading you undertake. If you deposit $100, and follow correct risk management protocols, you'll be able to solely risk ten pips if you're taking a one small heap position. This forces you to be a lively day merchant, whether or not you wish to day trade or not. With a ten pip stop loss you won't be ready to swing trade or invest, since the value will simply move ten pips against you, leading to a losing trade, if you are attempting to carry out for long gains.

New traders are more contented saving up extra money before gap a forex account, so adequately funding their account so that they will trade properly.

How Much cash do I want to Day Trade Forex?

If you wish to day trade Forex, I like to recommend gap associate degree account with a minimum of $2000, ideally $5000 if you wish a good financial gain stream.

With a $3000 account, and risking no quite 1 Chronicles of your account on every trade ($30 or less), you'll be able to build $60+ per day. With a $5000 account, you'll be able to risk up to $50 per trade, and so you'll be able to fairly build a median profit of $100+ per day.

This is doable as a result of let's say you risk concerning ten pips per trade, thus you'll be able to take a foothold size of concerning five mini tons ($1 per pip movement), which is able to lose you $50 or cause you to concerning $75 if your average gain is fifteen pips. In fact you won't win each trade, however if you win three out of five, you've created yourself $125 for the day. Some days you create additional, and a few days you create less.

So with a $5000 account you'll be able to begin to make a good stream of daily financial gain. If you permit the account to grow to $10,000 you'll be able to build roughly $250 per day. These are simply estimates of course; an improved estimate of your income potential can come from active in a very demo account, and watching your results before even risking one real dollar.

It is doable to start out associate degree account with a smaller quantity, like $500, however if doing thus build a commitment to grow the account for a minimum of a year before retreating any cash. If you are doing this, and don't risk quite 1 Chronicles of your account on every trade, you'll be able to build concerning $10 per day to start with, that over the course of a year can bring your account up to many thousand bucks.

How Much cash do I want to Swing Trade Forex?

Swing commercialism is once you hold positions for a few days to a couple weeks. This form of forex commercialism is suited to those who don't like watching their charts perpetually and/or who will solely trade their spare time.

With swing commercialism you're making an attempt to capture long term moves and so may have to carry positions through some gyrations (ups and downs) before the market really gets to your profit spot. A profit target could be a determined exit purpose for taking profits. For swing commercialism you'll typically have to be compelled to risk between twenty and one hundred pips on a trade, counting on your strategy and also the forex combine you're commercialism (some are additional volatile than others). Your expected profit ought to larger than the chance.

If wish to require a trade that has fifty pips of risk, absolutely the minimum you'll be able to open an account with is $500. This is often as a result of you'll be able to risk $5 per trade that is eighteen of $500. If you're taking a 1 small heap position ($0.10 per pip movement, and also the smallest position size possible) and lose fifty pips you'll be down $5. Since trades occur each couple days, you're doubtless to solely build concerning $10 or $12 per week. At this rate it might take variety of years to induce the account up to many thousand bucks.

If you begin with $5000, you'll be able to build concerning $100 to $120 per week that is additional of associate degree financial gain stream. With a $10,000 account you'll be able to doubtless snag a $200+ per week. Counting on wherever you reside, this might function associate degree adequate aspect financial gain. Again, this is often associate degree estimate. Observe in a very demo account for a few months before commercialism with real cash, as which will offer you a small amount higher plan of your financial gain potential. Demo commercialism is less complicated than real trading although, as a result of you've got nothing to lose.

Only have a $1000 (or less) to swing trade or day trade.

How Much Capital For Longer-Term Forex Trades/Investing?

The same risk management ideas apply to longer-term trades, which suggests risk ought to be unbroken to twenty or less of the account. With swing commercialism and day trading risking 1 Chronicles is nice, however with longer-term trades I don't mind risking a pair of. In my Forex ways Course for Weekly Charts, that discusses ways for taking trades that generally last for a month to many months (or typically longer), I like to recommend starting with a minimum of $4,000 in capital. This is often as a result of after we attempt to capture larger value moves we regularly have to be compelled to place our stop loss any removed from the entry purpose.

With this form of commercialism we have a tendency to could have stop losses that are three hundred or five hundred pips from our entry...but over the course of a few months we expect to create 1500 pips (for example). Even commercialism one small heap (approximately $0.10 per pip of movement), with a three hundred pip stop loss we have a tendency to are risking $30 if we lose. So as to risk $30 on a trade we want associate degree account balance of a minimum of $3000, if risking 1 Chronicles per trade (because 1 Chronicles of $3000 is $30). If you're willing to risk a pair of per trade, then $1500 in capital is required (because a pair of of $1500 is $30).

When commercialism completely different pairs with different trade setups, we have a tendency to could find yourself with trades that need a bigger (or smaller) stop loss. This is often why it's smart to deposit additional capital than less. Supported the instance on top of, a merchant could assume that $1500 is enough for longer-term commercialism in forex. It would be, however what if volatility will increase and most of the trades you see need a five hundred or 600 pip stop loss? With $1500, you're about to need to risk an excessive amount of of your account on every trade, even once taking only 1 small heap (the smallest position size). You'll prefer to not trade, then again you'll miss out on some nice opportunities. Begin with extra money in your account than you expect you'll would like, that manner you'll be able to trade with bigger confidence knowing that your risk is correctly controlled.

The beginning balance conjointly affects our financial gain potential. With a $4000 balance, taking trades that last a few months, an affordable financial gain estimate is $80 to $200 per month if risking 1 Chronicles of the account per trade (over time we are going to accumulate multiple positions, with some doubtless being opened and closed every month). If risking a pair of per trade that financial gain estimate doubles (assuming a profitable strategy is being used). Double the beginning balance, to $8000, and also the financial gain in bucks doubles once more.

How Much cash Do I want to Trade Forex

It is vital to be realistic concerning what you expect from your Forex trading. The amount of money you deposit plays a vital role in how much you'll doubtless build if you follow correct risk management. If you're willing to grow your account slowly, then you'll be able to doubtless begin with as very little as $500, however beginning with a minimum of a $1000 is suggested despite what form of commercialism you are doing. If you wish to create associate degree financial gain from your forex commercialism then i like to recommend gap an account with a minimum of $3000 for day trading, or $4000 for swing commercialism or finance. Play with the eventualities to seek out associate degree financial gain level and deposit level that's acceptable.

Most unsuccessful traders risk way more than a pair of of their account on one trade; this isn't suggested. It's doable for even nice traders and great ways to witness a series of losses. If you risk 100 percent of your account and lose six trades in a very row (which will happen) you've got considerably depleted your capital and currently you have to trade cleanly simply to induce back to even. If you risk only one or a pair of of your account on every trade, six losses is nothing. Most you capital is unbroken, you're ready to recoup your losses simply, and are back to creating a profit in no time.

The on top of eventualities assume that your average profit are going to be concerning one.5 times your risk (or greater), which you'll win concerning sixty % of your trades. This is often not invariably simple to accomplish systematically. Your personal commercialism trend can for the most part confirm your gain or lack of it. Though, what quantity cash you trade forex with can play a major role in your ability to fulfill your commercialism goals.

WHAT IS PASSIVE FINANCIAL GAIN

Passive financial gain is frequently generated cash that needs lowest effort on the part of the recipient to earn and maintain it. Gains on stocks, interest, commodities, lottery winnings and capital gains are typically the categories of earnings that return to mind.

However, while the on top of fits the favored definition of passive financial gain, some countries conjointly impose an additional technical definition for the aim of taxation. Nuances around such tax determinations are going to be elaborate any below.

Active Vs Passive commercialism

Active commercialism

People typically raise whether or not stock commercialism is passive financial gain. However, the solution can rely on your individual approach. Active traders can invest a substantial quantity of your time and energy into turning a profit. In fact, their trade activity can typically be their primary focus.

Passive commercialism

Whereas, if you're wanting to get a passive financial gain from day commercialism, you almost certainly don't will pay all day at your pc watching the markets and creating trades. In contrast to active traders, your passive financial gain can work around your life-style, instead of dictate it.

So, if you wish to get passive financial gain from options or bitcoin commercialism, for instance, you'll wish at handover your capital to a trusty broker, machine-controlled system or invest via copy commercialism.

Pros & Cons of Passive financial gain

Before we glance at some techniques and tips to earning passive income through day trade, it's vital you learn the advantages and downsides. The restricted quantity of your time you'll have to be compelled to commit is an understandable profit. However, this conjointly implies that there's exaggerated pressure on the investment selections you are doing build.

In addition, passive commercialism will typically end in a slower stream of profit compared to active trading. There's conjointly a danger that you just can neglect watching your passive financial gain. This will end in losing out on potential profits. Instead, you'll pay most time worrying concerning your positions that you just too interfere, limiting returns.

How to Generate Passive financial gain

Automation

To make day trade passive financial gain simple, some intercommunicate automation. Used properly, machine-controlled systems could modify you to get substantial profits. This is often as a result of there's solely a particular variety of trades you'll be able to manually build day after day. Whereas a complicated rule will mechanically enter and exit positions as presently as pre-determined criteria are met.

They conjointly modify you to trade variety of markets quickly. In fact, once you've got programmed in your criteria, you'll be able to generate passive financial gain while you're sleeping.

Some could clearly doubt the effectivity of those systems. However, close to seventy fifth of all trades created on the big apple exchange and also the NASDAQ currently originate from these algorithms, demonstrating their capabilities.

Software

Before you'll be able to start developing a passive financial gain through machine-controlled stocks commercialism, for instance, you'll have to be compelled to notice the proper computer code. Do your analysis and check reviews before you invest in any.

Once you've got a selected computer code, you'll have to be compelled to develop an efficient strategy. Making a list of your day commercialism parameters is usually a decent place to start out. You'll wish to think about the following:

- once to enter and exit positions
- Position size
- Intraday commercialism timeframe
- Targets and stop-losses

Algorithm

Once you've develop a method, you'll have to be compelled to have the rule written. If you've got some technical data you'll be ready to input directions yourself, because the code is comparatively easy. However, if not, you'll wish to think about hiring a computer user to help you.

Back-Testing

Before you'll be able to use an automatic system to get a passive financial gain with bitcoin, for instance, you'll conjointly have to be compelled to back take a look at your strategy. This enables you take a look at your system before you risk any capital. You just run your computer code against historical value knowledge to induce a gauge for the way well it performs. You'll be able to then establish and remedy any problems.

The Monte Carlo simulation could be a useful gizmo to do. This repeatedly tests steps of your rule and inputs random knowledge into your parameters. This can permit you to forecast however well your new system goes to perform.

Application

With the labor hopefully done, you'll be able to now get pleasure from looking at that passive financial gain build up in your account. However, you'll have to be compelled to habitually check your computer code is performing arts for sure. Technical glitches and anomalies will occur.

Copy Trading

Arguably, differently for commercialism passive financial gain to be created simple is thru copy trading. Instead of devoting right smart time and energy into developing a method and watching the markets, you'll be able to take pleasure in the success of toughened traders.

You simply opt for a merchant and so a program can mimic that trader's shopping for and commercialism along with your capital. However, typically you'll notice the traders and also the website will take a little share of your profit. In fact, those that imitate traders can even then be traced and earn commissions.

A broker like eToro focuses on social copy commercialism.

Drawbacks

You may be thinking this is often the perfect thanks to begin forex commercialism as passive financial gain. However, whether or not its stocks, futures or forex, there stay sure drawbacks to consider:

• Risking capital – you need to be ready that thanks to the volatility of markets, you'll lose all the capital you at the start invested with. If you're notably risk-averse, seeing giant losses for a few of days could even stop you sleeping.

• selecting a merchant – selecting a trader isn't any easy challenge. For instance, associate degree aggressive crypto merchant could clear you go in many days. So, contemplate their instrument of selection and approach. Also, check their recent trade history. You wish steady and consistent results. It's value noting, however, some people really notice many toughened traders to repeat.

• Not Following Trades proportionately – Some sites might not permit you to trade proportionally. However, for good, if not clear reasons, traders typically invest specific quantities. So, confirm you actually follow repetition your merchant.

• Learning tool vs secured cash generator – several argue trade repetition is best used as a tool by beginners to find out concerning completely different markets and instruments. So, bear in mind it should not be the most effective means that to get a passive financial gain day commercialism.

Overall, for those fascinated by day commercialism for passive financial gain, you'll wish to think about each strategies on top of. Every might considerably cut back the number of your time you've got to pay intraday commercialism. However, it's conjointly value highlight they are available with drawbacks and risks. Therefore, the challenge is deciding which is able to fit your individual desires and life-style.

Passive financial gain & Taxes

Before you choose day commercialism is that the right manner for you to get a passive financial gain, there are sure rules and rules value considering. Some tax systems split earning sorts into 3 distinct categories:

• Passive – typically thought of internet income and income from a business during which the payer doesn't materially participate. It can even embody self-charged interest. This definition encompasses a broad vary of activities. To make up this bracket you need to not be too concerned in your intraday trade activities.

• Portfolio – Capital gains from securities and commodities commercialism, like stocks, currencies, gold, ETFs, etc., is often thought of portfolio financial gain. However, it should or might not even be thought of passive financial gain.

• Active – because the name suggests, you need to be unendingly and well involved the endeavor. If you were to pay most of your day engaged in intraday commercialism, for instance, you'd make up this class.

These definitions vary to some extent as you progress between completely different taxes jurisdictions. The point, however, is that it's informed check what sort of trade activity can represent passive financial gain wherever you reside, and whether or not there any specific tax rules you wish to bear in mind.

Many countries contemplate passive financial gain nonexempt like non-passive income. However, it can even be treated otherwise. For instance, in the US, the government agency permits passive losses to be written off solely against passive gains. So, once losses exceed the financial gain from passive day trading activities, the remainder of the loss are often carried forward to the consequent tax year, as long as there's some passive financial gain to jot down it off against.

Of course passive financial gain are a few things the general public would really like. Who wouldn't just like the plan of earning cash while you're out having a good time?

Fortunately, trendy technology currently permits people to some extent, to require a back seat and still manufacture a profit. However, you need to notice a system that suits your individual circumstances, whereas conjointly considering the risks and any tax rules.

MANAGED FOREX ACCOUNT VERSUS AUTOMATED TRADING SOFTWARE FOR MAKING PASSIVE FINANCIAL GAIN

Unless you've got been living below a rock over the past few years you have seen unnumbered numbers of programs, seminars, courses, eBooks and T.V commercials touting the advantages of learning the way to trade the exchange Currency Market -"Forex". Within the thick of the info there looks to be a practical ability for those that invest the time to find out sound ways and techniques to get consistent profits through this vehicle. Wherever a drag arises is through the abundance of ads, promotions and promoting messages that arrange to persuade customers that there's some secret Forex commercialism computer code or very little notable Forex commercialism System which will build taking advantage of the Forex Market a straightforward task.

The reality is despite the plug the sole viable choice for "Easy Forex Profits" was through a Managed Forex commercialism account. This is often wherever someone who has no interest in learning the way to become a prolific merchant merely deposits funds into a Forex commercialism Account and signs a restricted Power Of professional person giving the rights to create selections on what trades are going to be placed on his account to a seasoned Forex merchant. The advantages of this sort of arrangement appear terribly obvious, the capitalist will merely pay their time as they opt for, the merchant to get access to additional funds to trade with and also the trader receives a management fee of somewhere between 20-35% of the profits in most cases. Here are many of the drawbacks.

A) The merchant, though solely being paid once he makes a profit, doesn't lose something once he loses the investors' cash on a trade or series of trades. He will really "experiment" with new trading ways etc. if he selected to with no repercussions as a result of he's not using his own cash to trade with!

B) Typically the minimum price to induce involved a Managed Forex Trading Account is $50,000.00. There are some with minimums as low as $10,000.00, however, even that's a stretch for many individuals. This truth alone prohibits access to the present choice from smaller investors.

C) you've got zero input into the kind of risk per trade, what currency pairs are being listed etc. most managed accounts merely trade your account and don't wish or welcome any input from you. Additionally, you typically need to get permission to withdraw your own money!

Now let's look into another that modified the foundations. I think this feature is an additional viable choice to a Managed Forex commercialism Account. It's referred to as machine-controlled Forex commercialism computer code. There are several options to decide on from like FAP Turbo, Forex Megadroid, Trend Trimmer, Forex Funnel and additional however the common thread is that they will simply be downloaded and put in on any MetaTrader4 platform obtainable at the most brokers. It typically takes but ten minutes to line up a computer code of your selection and inside minutes you'll be able to have the software process knowledge to require trades on a live or demo account.

Unlike the Managed Forex commercialism Accounts the machine-controlled Forex commercialism computer code permits you the subsequent flexibility.

A) You'll be able to invest as very little as $500 with ANY broker WHO offers the MetaTrader4 Platform.

B) There's NO management fee charged to your account by any traders thus you retain 100 percent of the profits they create you.

C) You'll be able to change from conservative or aggressive as you wish the computer code to be, otherwise you can merely opt for the default settings then set it and forget it.

In addition, with most Managed Forex Trading Accounts you've got restrictions on once and the way a lot of of YOUR cash you'll be able to withdraw. Once you use a Forex commercialism computer code YOU management once and the way a lot of you wish to withdraw from your account and also the software mechanically adjusts to atone for it.

D) Most Forex computer code conjointly referred to as Forex Robots, are typically offered through a payment processor like ClickBank. This enables you to induce paid to refer others if you select. There are only a few if any managed forex commercialism accounts which will pay you a referral fee for sharing it with others.

The computer code choice, in my opinion, could be a higher option than the managed commercialism account to make consistent passive financial gain particularly if you are doing not have loads of cash. Your primary goal once trying to make passive financial gain or passive residual income is to stay expenses low or to own no current expenses in any respect with the potential for profits high. If you had $50000 invested with in a well-managed Forex trading account and you're paying a half-hour performance fee to your merchant and also the come for the month was five-hitter. Your potential profit would be $1500-30% that is $450.00. Your income would be $1050.00. If the profits remained at this level monthly you'd be sacrificing over $5000 p.a. in passive income! i feel the selection is pretty clear, grab yourself an automatic forex commercialism computer code.

PASSIVE FINANCIAL GAIN THROUGH FOREX TRADING COURSES

Although so many dream of one day becoming "made" not many will achieve this. Unfortunately, a regular job will not help one achieve this. Having a business and an everyday job can help to bring in a considerable amount of extra cash. However, there's a chance to become "made" through trading currency which is referred to as Forex trading. There are various business opportunities obtainable on-line and plenty of Forex commercialism courses you'll be able to learn from.

Some of the "Get made quick" schemes are bound to be scams. However, Forex trading grants informative trading product that assist you earn a passive financial gain. You simply have to be compelled to have the drive to earn cash and to pay a minimum of twenty minutes on a daily basis to find out and apply the Forex trading technique provided. Forex commercialism courses have piecemeal trading strategies designed by Forex mentors acknowledge within the Forex market.

The Forex market is one wherever you wish to face frequent ups and downs. If you are doing not have enough data, you'll tend to lose cash. However, the Forex commercialism course allows you to find out the techniques by defrayal simply twenty minutes daily. The correct foretelling will assist you earn a passive financial gain by applying what's learned.

Swing trading is one more trading trend completely designed for stock trading. The exchange is taken into account to be a risky investment by many folks. This is often owing to the actual fact that several individuals lose cash available commercialism. However, the most reason for losing is thanks to their inability to know the short moves of the trade. You'll be able to earn a passive financial gain available market through smart exchange courses.

The top quality exchange courses disclose the ways and techniques that assist you conclude at that purpose the market faces change. Once you've got learned the techniques to face these unexpected changes, you'll be able to get nice edges from this market. The course allows you to find out the commercialism technique although you're a beginner.

ETF is one more effective trading technique that helps you earn nice financial gain from the Exchange listed Fund markets. ETF permits you to trade like stock and it are often listed intraday. You'll be able to save cash by finance in ETF market provided you recognize the techniques of the trade. You'll be able to get pleasure from additional blessings sort of a low turnover and broad diversification. It's vital to recollect that ETF could be a trade that runs through brokerage corporations and every trade needs commission charges.

Home study Forex trading courses ought to help you learn about Forex trading. The courses ought to be designed to be used any time and for any market state of affairs. In fact, the pliability of the course ought to be its main feature. It ought to be simple to learn and follow. The Forex trading course ought to embody sensible points and provide clear examples for victorious learning thus you're so ready to apply the strategies merely. Following the course printed and demo commercialism fruitfully you'll be able to begin generating a considerable financial gain from your investments.

Most of those who fail in online business lack cash management skills. The commercialism product from smart forex mentors teach you strategies of trading in associate degree easy-to-understand manner. Hence, you're ready to earn a passive financial gain with applied ways. The courses offered by commercialism mentors ought to assist you choose inexpensive brokerage corporations and acquire you started trading.

Making financial gains in trading - FACTS to think about

Several recessions worldwide have already weakened personal finances to a great extend and thence individuals are wanting to develop an extra earning supply which will act as an ingenious passive earning source. Nowadays, affiliate promoting, serving as a contract online and forex promoting are thought of as convenient passive financial gain generation resources.

Among all, forex is one among the strategies that don't would like specific skills to get a pile of money; rather a transparent monetary construct will get you the profit through a completely machine-controlled system. Let's explore many ways that to earn passively from forex commercialism.

Ways to create passive financial gain in forex trading: facts you need to explore

* Forex is one among the trade dealing markets that run globally 24/7 except Saturdays and Sundays (bank holidays). Despite wherever you're trading from, you're invariably connected to the international market. If you analyze the trends, you'll automatically perceive the way to invest and attain a growth of concerning ten % anytime you purchase or sell.

* Build and maintain active social profiles to induce forex signals earlier. These social signals can assist you decide concerning consequent steps, the foremost potential investments. Step by step you'll learn the way to require call by yourself and reap most profit.

* Recently a replacement plan has return up. Repetition different victorious traders has invariably been the most effective plan for the newbies. Nowadays, leading forex brokers like eToro are functioning on machine-controlled trading computer code. Using these machine-controlled tools, one will copy the victorious investors and build the whole operation automatically. If you don't have enough time to pay on Forex traders, think about employing these tools to setup the foremost economical passive earning generator.

Start trading within the Forex market - easy steps explained below:

1. First, you've got to open a trading account with a forex broker online. The platform can assist you to connect with the market. At an equivalent time, the platform takes care of your transactions charging commonplace fees.

2. Next, you've got to deposit some cash into your account. Most brokers have a restriction and you need to need to deposit the minimum quantity asked by the brokers.

3. Next, you'll be able to begin commercialism online. The cash you've got deposited are going to be thought of as your investment and employed in the commercialism.

4. You'll be able to copy the market leaders and follow the machine-controlled method. Most leading Forex brokers have already developed a compact system to create the commercialism operation easier and profitable for the new traders.

5. If you wish to trade on Forex regularly, you'll be able to analyze the signals and trends. This can assist you to become the market leader and enhance your profit considerably.

Warnings: Forex are often a good technique to line up your dream passive earning supply. Don't take this as a regular profession unless you've got a decent quantity of cash to gamble. It'll be nice if you begin functioning on Forex, learn the fundamentals and so on before even thinking about quitting your job.

GENERATING PASSIVE INCOME WITHOUT BEING AN EXPERT TRADER

Foreign exchange commercialism refers to 1 of the most important markets round the world. This clearly makes huge financial gain for several individuals. However, for the knowledgeable traders it's fairly simple to create cash here as they perceive the trends. However the new traders notice it extremely tough and finish losing cash sometimes too! As luck would have it, today, there are loads of Forex marketplaces where you'll be able to really learn trading from the consultants and begin creating cash although you're a beginner. Even the beginners will currently begin creating passive financial gain from Forex trading online. There are some specific steps you must follow and you actually have to be compelled to understand what you're doing. Here you'll explore the way to build passive financial gain from Forex trading while not being associate degree knowledgeable and toughened merchant from home. The steps are simple and easy to follow!

How to generate passive financial gain from forex trading like an expert?

There are various ways that you'll be able to build passive financial gain from Forex trading. You'll be able to do your own analysis, get some suggestions from the market leaders, using forex robots or repetition the steps of the most effective traders on the platform. If you wish to create cash actively, you've got additional options; except for those that wish to create cash in a very passive mode has got to follow the opposite strategies for automation. Here you'll find out about the machine-controlled systems:

#1 conclude additional concerning the market leaders

First of all, it's important to seek out the market leaders. There are so many of those who claim that they're creating a lot of cash as associate degree knowledgeable merchant, however solely many of them are creating the proper selections all the time. You've got to seek out these market leaders and acquire connected with them. Once you get the chance to require a sneak-peek into what they're doing, you're halfway done. Thus noticing your leaders or mentors is that the first and most significant step! Take enough time to analysis and find the most effective mentor for yourself.

#2 copy them, however don't act blind!

As you've found your mentor, it's time to mimic their actions. There are many computer code and platforms which will assist you copy their traders while not even work into your account. You'll be able to simply copy their trades and build cash equally as them. You'll be able to merely build loads of cash once you've got a good merchant to follow. However, you shouldn't act blindly and follow the ever-changing tides all the time. This can prevent surprising hazards!

#3 keep updated and determined!

Finally, you've got to stay updated and determined concerning creating cash. As there are variant opportunities during this field, you've got to stay to your arrange and focus. You wish to remain updated and centered towards creating cash. Although you didn't earn the cash you planned for, you can't afford to step back. Rather you've got to stay updated and build changes in your ways consequently.

USING FOREX MANAGED ACCOUNTS ON SMALL INVESTMENTS

Small forex managed accounts are ideal for the investors WHO have some preoccupations and can't observe or trade in the market themselves.

Traders WHO are engaged in jobs and still searching for ways to enter the Forex market but do not want to spend hours on the pc, can open a Forex managed account for passive financial gain. In a market wherever over 2 trillion in currency is listed on a daily basis, a managed Forex account earn massive profits for you.

Forex managed accounts are managed by a merchant. There are 2 kinds of managed forex accounts--either machine-controlled or managed by human traders or brokers.

Automated tiny forex managed accounts are fully automatic programs that are designed by toughened traders and supply unmatched simplicity to the investors. It takes into account all indicators and statistics available to it and once it receives a sign, it trades consequently. However, these systems lack the human intelligence and instinct that without doubt play a very important role in decision-making.

The second sort of Forex managed accounts workers human traders with market expertise of the many years.

The typical investment in a very tiny managed forex account are often from $5,000 to $10,000, which leaves the terribly tiny investors out of the loop. A managed account that is either listed by another person or an automatic system will earn up to 20% per month or additional counting on the performance of the system.

Small managed forex accounts are the most effective choice before you leap into the market if you're receiving skilled coaching and getting ready yourself and on the way to trade in the market. You'll be able to fine-tune your own trading system and techniques and learn the way the market could respond to specific news and patterns.

Searching for a decent managed tiny forex account could be a hard task. Some commercialism systems could take too several trades inflicting you to margin out timely and a few may generate poor signals. Confirm that the trading system will substantiate its knowledge with tried results and perform back tests on their system for periods of time. The broker you selected should be established, registered, and has quality inside the market.

Many brokers supply their services for tiny managed forex accounts for personal or individual investors. They'll supply some preferences for top investments for portfolio diversification and effective risk management. The brokerage corporations have pool of toughened monetary advisors who will give ready-made, glorious and even customized solutions in commercialism and programs for you. Your tiny investment could also be clubbed along with different investments to earn the sort of profit you're searching for with substantial risk management procedures.

Your tiny managed Forex account becomes operative the instant you authorize your broker to require investment selections on your behalf and they may start to manage your funds. The benefits of employing a tiny managed forex account to trade are –

1. You do not wish to trade yourself .

2. You are not influenced by trading emotions.

3. Lesser possibilities of making mistakes, particularly thus with machine-controlled forex.

4. You invest tiny amounts but receive high returns with correct risk management facilities.

www.ingramcontent.com/pod-product-compliance
Lightning Source LLC
Chambersburg PA
CBHW062109220526
45471CB00010B/3660